It has not been my foolish ambition to give a full-scale picture of the Resistance. All I have been able to do has been to lift one corner of the veil and afford a glimpse of the throbbing life and the suffering in the midst of the battle.

JOSEPH KESSEL.

London, Kinnerton Studio.
September 8, 1943.

JOSEPH KESSEL

ARMY
OF SHADOWS

TRANSLATED BY

RAINER J. HANSHE

INTRODUCTION BY

STUART KENDALL

Contra Mundum Press   New York · London · Melbourne

Translation *L'Armée des ombres*
© 2017 Rainer J. Hanshe;
introduction © 2017 Stuart
Kendall

First Contra Mundum Press
Edition 2017.

Library of Congress
Cataloguing-in-Publication Data

Kessel, Joseph, 1898–1979
[*L'Armée des ombres*. English.]

Army of Shadows / Joseph Kessel;
translated from the French by
Rainer J. Hanshe

—1st Contra Mundum Press
Edition
314 pp., 5 x 8 in.

ISBN 9781940625225

   I. Kessel, Joseph.
  II. Title.
 III. Hanshe, Rainer J.
 IV. Translator.
  V. Stuart Kendall.
 VI. Introduction.

2017940108

TABLE OF CONTENTS

INTRODUCTION

WHEN FACT BECOMES LEGEND

STUART KENDALL

Plato famously proposed banning poets from his ideal Republic. Poetry and the arts in general offer nothing but imitations of the things of the world, he argued, and therefore serve no useful purpose. Worse, poetry might incite the passions and spread fear and delusion among those who can least endure such things. Plato: "If he believes in the reality of the underworld and its terrors, do you think that any man will be fearless of death and in battle will prefer death to defeat and slavery?" Rather, if there are to be tales of death, let the poets praise it, he says, among those who would be warriors.[1] Plato's points are well taken. Real factual or philosophical understanding rarely motivates action. Poetry on the other hand excels at just such an incitement. How then might literary or poetic works best be used to motivate or incite action? What in short might be an effective politics of poetry?

Joseph Kessel's *Army of Shadows* offers a potent example. As a portrait of resistance in France during World War Two, it was written to serve essentially propagandistic purposes, to help, in its way, the Free French win the war. But the book proposes neither a hymn to the gods nor a simple or straightforward celebration of "good men", of the kind that might have appealed to Plato. Rather, the occasionally bewildering space Kessel explores is simultaneously that of moral outrage *and* moral compromise. Moreover, Kessel presents the book as both factual and, in a curious way, fictional, as a work of literature. The book, in short, embodies many things at once, held often in uneasy balance. Reading it now, almost 75 years after it was written, presents further problems, though also new opportunities for reflection on these themes.

Anglophone literature has no one quite like Joseph Kessel: a writer as well-known for his contributions to the front pages of newspapers as for his novels, whose works were equally successful with critics and readers. The popular success of his writing assured his financial security though he was equally as devoted to spending money as to earning it. Indeed, Kessel, commonly known as Jef, was almost as famous for his appetites as for his artistic achievements. One of his biographers, Yves Courrière, once witnessed him consume twenty-seven scotches in six hours. The man lost vast sums in casinos; smoked opium for years with, among others, his close friend, Jean Cocteau; & passed his nights bouncing between wives and lovers. A natural raconteur and *bon vivant*, Kessel was a colossus of narrative energy and raw life bursting off the page; his biography seems stitched together from extraordinary events and impossible chance encounters. His books — almost always topical bestsellers of moral and political import — also inspired a few enduring cinematic masterpieces of his century — *Army of Shadows*, certainly, but also *Belle de Jour* — while his dialogue for *Mayerling* (directed by his friend Anatole Litvak) helped launch the career of Charles Boyer and thereby too, Kessel's own career writing for film. But Kessel's very success spoiled him for some critics, who never quite took him seriously, even as he was nominated for and perhaps begrudgingly admitted to the high temple of French *belles lettres*, the prestigious Académie Française in 1962. The previous year he had covered — along with Hannah Arendt & other reporters addressing the conscience of the world — the trial of Adolf Eichmann in Jerusalem for *France-Soir*. At the center of it all, his writing: some eighty books — novels, stories, biographies, memoirs, and of course short & long-form journalism — bear his name. Kessel's life as a journalist, novelist, traveler, adventurer, and public spectacle bridged many spheres, while being at once symptomatic or representative of many faces of modernity, as a clash of civilizations, media, and mores.

Three cultures came together in Kessel's formation: French, Russian, and Jewish; each tangled in contradiction and tempered by a restlessly cosmopolitan regard for humanity. Jewish in the time of modern, cosmopolitan emancipation;

Russian in the time of Soviet hegemony and the exile of dissent; French in the time — chronicled in *Army of Shadows* — of international conflict & the political collapse of France itself, the epoch wherein France became a contentious idea rather than an actual territory, a moral entity rather than a political one and when even that — faced with the self-inflicted wounds of colonialism — faltered.

The author's father, Chmouel Kessel, was born to Orthodox Jewish parents in Lithuania in 1866. He came to France in 1885 to study medicine, first in Paris, later in Montpellier. As part of the process of assimilation, he changed his name to Samuel. The author's mother, Raïssa, was Russian, from Orenbourg, and passionate about theater, though she too came west to study medicine, first in Geneva, then in Montpellier, where she and Samuel met. They married in Orenbourg in 1895 and emigrated to Argentina in 1896, under the continued sponsorship of Baron Maurice de Hirsch, who previously paid for Samuel's medical studies. Joseph Kessel was born in Argentina on January 31, 1898. The family did not, however, stay in South America for long. The following year they moved, first to Orenbourg and then, discovering that Samuel's French medical certificates were invalid in Russia, back to France by 1901. Nevertheless, within four years, they would return to Russia again, Samuel having at this point completed medical studies recognized there. Though still a child, young Joseph absorbed the world of Russia during these years, its language, music, customs, and superstitions, as well as its modes of work and play. Throughout his life,

Kessel would always return to Russian restaurants and bars with their music and community in exile, as sources of relaxation, places he felt at home.

By 1908, however, the family was once again in France, this time in Nice, which better suited Samuel's health, damaged years earlier by tuberculosis. When they moved to Paris, in 1913, it was to provide access to the best schools for Kessel and his two younger brothers, Lazare (nicknamed Lola) and Georges. Kessel attended lycée Louis-le-Grand & later the Sorbonne, by which point he was deeply involved in literary and dramatic arts, writing and performing plays with his brother, Lola. In 1915, while still pursuing his license at the Sorbonne, Kessel began writing for *Journal des Débats*, primarily, at first, about Russia & related topics.

World War I accelerated rather than interrupted Kessel's life trajectory. Though a Russian national, he enlisted on the side of the French. With his diploma in hand, he was given a position as an officer in an aviation corps stationed outside of Rheims at the front. As a machine gunner, and while providing information for directing artillery, he discovered a love of flight that would persist throughout his life. Back at the barracks, amid the close community created by the shared dangers and traumas of combat, Kessel also indulged in two other passions that would become persistent and occasionally debilitating, those for drink and gambling. During the closing days of the war, Kessel volunteered to be part of a special, multinational squadron intended to back up the allied White Russian Army in its war in Europe and with the Bolsheviks, from the rear, via Vladivostok. The mission began with a trip, by land, sea, and air, around the world, from France, across North America, from New York to San Francisco, to Hawai'i, Manila, on to Japan, and ultimately Russia. By chance, the war ended just as the aviators arrived in New York, turning their intended pressing military voyage into a victory tour, showered with the full gratitude — and thus also inevitably debauched revels — in each city they traversed. When Kessel finally reached Siberia, his knowledge of the Russian language led him to be drafted into an operation securing supply train wagons for an army of essentially marauding Cossacks. His eventual trip home took him through ports on the China Sea, the Indian Ocean, and the Red Sea. He smoked opium for the first time in Shanghai and met his first wife, Nadia-Alexandra Polizu-Michsunesti, known as Sandi, on the voyage.

Kessel would return again and again to his experiences during these few turbulent years as fecund sources for novels and stories. But the habits for excess he adopted during this period of almost relentless travel and adventure, as well as drink and drug-fueled excesses, would also continue to characterize his life for years to come. Toward the end of his life, Kessel looked back:

> During a long period of my life that lasted almost forty years, I obeyed my instincts & my desires before everything else, in a sometimes excessive, sometimes too excessive way. With gambling, alcohol, with drugs,

it was the same. Life is the same thing. There's no pride or shame in it. I've always accepted the risks.[2]

Or again, as part of the same conversation:

This violent, imperious need to take risks to infringe upon norms, to push myself to the limits of every situation, as if to push back the limits of the impossible; I experienced this need that carried me to live the frenzy of the Russian bars, even to the point of delirium, when very young.[3]

More or less as soon as Kessel returned to France in 1919, the patterns and practices of his life were established. Rather than settle into the life of a university professor, as his parents hoped, Kessel picked up his nascent career as a journalist and writer, beginning where he left off with the *Journal des Débats*, but quickly moving on, publishing journalism, interviews, and stories in an ever widening range of newspapers and other publications as his contacts and reputation grew: *Le Mercure de France*, *La Liberté*, *Le Figaro*, *La Revue de France*, *Revue des deux mondes*, *Le Matin*, and many others. In the early and mid-1920s, alongside other topics and locales, Kessel covered both the Irish Civil War and the mounting unrest in Palestine, as well as continuing to write about Russia in the aftermath of the Revolution. His journalism became the enduring bedrock upon which he grounded his fiction. He saw himself as being part of a literary tradition in which journalism & literary writing, as he said in an interview, "complete one another, [&] are tightly linked. This is the line of Conrad, of Kipling, of Stevenson, of Jack London. And in fact, where does journalism begin, or end? How many writers undertake long inquiries before writing a novel? All of Zola is journalism."[4] Graham Greene, George Orwell, and Ernest Hemingway are examples in Anglophone literature, from Kessel's own generation, of journalist-writers. But whereas Hemingway, for one, often regarded his journalism as an impediment to his literary career and as profoundly secondary to it, Kessel embraced this aspect of his vocation and pursued it consistently. Throughout his life, Kessel went wherever the stories were; he sought them out in tragedies, revolutions, and wars. In 1956, he published the first three of what would ultimately be seven substantial volumes of his selected journalism under the title *Témoin parmi les hommes* (Witness Among Men), but his bibliography also includes many other volumes of long-form journalism & biography as well.

Already in the early 1920s, when covering the Irish Civil War, Kessel had a strong sense of the moral purpose of reporting. Clear-headed & carefully observed journalism provides a necessary check on the potential delusions of political fanatics, whether on the left or the right.

> If a journalist is investigating passionate & often fanatical partisans, the responsibility of casting doubt on some of their affirmations enters into his job.

Good faith is not in question here, but the instinct for measure and a sense of precision. The effects of anger, of suffering, of passion, of blind support transmitted from father to son, the secular hatreds that feed the blood, ultimately the need, even unconscious, for propaganda, all of those inner forces come together to distort vision, to throw judgment off balance, and thereby to prevent a just appreciation of facts and actions.[5]

Kessel's journalism gave him topics but it also gave him techniques to use in his fiction. His journalistic style is nevertheless unlikely to be even recognizable as journalism to readers, particularly Anglophone readers, today. The author's voice and perspective is too present even as the stories themselves typically offer snapshots *in medias res*, often almost rushing past, close enough to the action to be caught up in it. Whether in Ireland or Israel, Germany, Spain, Syria, Morocco, Hollywood, Kenya, or Afghanistan, or for that matter many other places around the globe, Kessel stays almost impossibly, even myopically close to individual people and their perspectives on the events that engulf and too often overwhelm them. He has an instinct and an ear for a good story, and, once heard, he knows how to tell one too; a feeling for the drama of situation, psychology, and telling detail. His journalism provides the facts from which one might gain a knowing perspective on current events rather than statements of that perspective itself. He doesn't tell his reader what to think, he places his reader in the emotional space of the drama.

As Yves Courrière put it in one among many memorable phrases, in his journalism, Kessel always put "people before politics, portraits before analysis, stories before History."[6] The pieces endure as deeply moving rushes cut from an abandoned film of his age. Though informative, these pieces still presented only fragments of the world. Kessel would use his literary writings, his stories and novels, to fill out those fragments in the form of character driven narratives.

This too began in the early 1920s, when he distilled his experiences as an aviator at the front into his first great literary success, *L'Équipage* (The Crew, 1923)[7], and the lessons learned from his coverage of the Irish Civil War into the novella *Mary de Cork* (1925). Gaston Gallimard, the founder of the eponymous publishing house, discovered Kessel's writing the way so many other readers did, in the pages of newspapers & magazines. He wrote to the author in 1922 & began an editorial relationship that would endure — with a break during the German occupation — until Kessel's death fifty-seven years later. With Gallimard as his publisher, the daily press as his platform, & his own irrepressible habits as a *bon vivant*, Kessel quickly developed deep & lasting friendships with the French literary establishment; fellow writers like Jean Cocteau, Raymond Radiguet (until his early death), & Colette were his companions from the early 1920s, though his circle expanded exponentially over the years.

Kessel came of age as a novelist in the 1920s alongside other popular literary writers of travel and adventure, Antoine de Saint-Exupéry & André Malraux perhaps most notably.

He would eventually befriend both of them. In terms of influence, alongside the literary journalists mentioned above, Kessel frequently listed among his inspirations the great Russian novelists, Dostoyevsky & Tolstoy, which he read in Russian, as well as Alexandre Dumas' *The Three Musketeers*, and the works of Malraux; finally Shakespeare, "the immense, the prodigious Shakespeare. He makes me dizzy with humility."[8] All of these influences testify to Kessel's interest in both popular success and serious intent, both of which certainly characterize his work.

The popular success of Kessel's books as well as their themes and settings of dramatic action all but inevitably invited their filmic adaptation. Seventeen films have been based on his works to date. *Belle de Jour* (dir. Louis Buñuel, 1966) and *Army of Shadows* (dir. Jean-Pierre Melville, 1969) are undoubtedly the most enduring, but Kessel's novel *L'Équipage* has been filmed three times. Kessel's own work in film began in 1935 when he started working with Anatole Litvak on the dialogue for the second film version of *L'Équipage*. As a result of that success, he travelled to Hollywood with Litvak in the late 1930s and continued to write for film — & later television — until the 1970s, penning scenarios & dialogue for feature films and narration for the documentaries that grew out of his work as a journalist.

Following his coverage of Russia in the aftermath of the revolution, the Irish Civil War, and the crisis in Palestine, it was all but inevitable that Kessel would chronicle the rise of Nazi Fascism in his journalism as well as treating the subject in a novel, *La Passante du Sans-Souci* (The Carefree Stroller, 1936), the story of a cabaret singer who falls into a life of drinking, drugs, and prostitution while attempting to support the man that she loves, a publisher placed in a concentration camp by the Nazi regime. He also covered the General Strike in Spain in 1934 and the Spanish Civil War in 1938. At the opposite pole of the political spectrum, since he was steeped in Russian traditional culture and close to the Russian exile community in Paris, it is unsurprising that Kessel did not embrace communism when it was fashionable for many members of his generation to do so. When the *Congrès international des écrivains* assembled in Paris in June 1935, Kessel stood apart. Yves Courrière describes Kessel as "too individualistic"[9] to be caught up in politics at the time, though perhaps more rightly Kessel's political stance should be understood, like his journalism, as rooted in his feeling for people rather than parties, and ultimately characterized as a politics of friendship. Nevertheless, though in keeping with this interpretation, as some members of the far right in France drifted into anti-Semitism, Kessel broke several close and long-standing friendships, including, most significantly, for him, with publishers, editors, and journalists like Henri Béraud *&* Horace de Carbuccia, whom he had known and worked with for many years.

In September 1939, when the Second World War began, Kessel, at the age of 41, returned to enlisted service. Given his vocation, his assignment was to continue his work as a journalist in uniform, as a war correspondent for *Paris-Soir*.

Pushing the bounds of his responsibility beyond the limits set by the military authorities, Kessel worked his way to the front line during the phony war and, nine months later, during the actual invasion, he again worked his way to the front, to be among the first to report the locations of the German troops as they swept through Champagne toward the capital. Through his contacts he was one of the only journalists permitted to make his way to Dunkirk during the flotilla that accompanied the catastrophic retreat of the French & British forces.

As France fell to the invading army, Kessel gathered his wife, Katia, and children, his mistress, Germaine, and his aging mother, Raïssa (his father had died of a heart attack in 1931, leaving Kessel as head of the family) to strategize about their future as Jews in occupied France. As a recognized and recognizably famous reporter and novelist who had already painted the Nazis in print with the most unflattering brush, Kessel wasn't likely to be safe in occupied Paris. His brother Georges was living in Hollywood at the time and encouraged Kessel to bring the family across the Atlantic, if not to Hollywood, at least to New York. Raïssa was too old to fear the Germans enough to flee. Kessel's longtime mistress, Germaine, went south, while Kessel & Katia initially fled to Lisbon for a few months, considering their options. Ultimately Katia would return to Paris with the children to look after their home while Kessel, after the armistice, would report for demobilization in Perpignan, in Vichy, and from there go to Marseille to support himself writing for the regional edition of *Paris-Soir*. His books, like those of other Jews *&* political commentators, had been banned by the Nazis in September 1940 as part of the Otto list.

Why did Kessel return to France? His triple heritage — French, Russian, Jewish — as well as his cosmopolitan love for travel might suggest that he could have easily joined the exodus of intellectuals *&* others who sought safety — and possibly a new kind of adventure — in New York or another foreign land. In 1952, during a radio interview with Dominque Fabre, Kessel explained:

> It was in 1940. As a war correspondent, I followed the retreat, the rout, the exodus on all the roads. And while passing through the countryside of Champagne, of Ile-de-France, of the Loire, and while thinking that those marvelous landscapes were soon going to be stomped by German troops, I cried for whole hours and I understood that France was my true country since I could not imagine that I could cry either for Russia or for Palestine.[10]

He wrote to his brother while still in Lisbon, "I am certain that I would be less unhappy hungry *&* cold and even afraid, persecuted in France, than comfortably settled in an apartment in New York or a house in Hollywood."[11]

These statements testify to Kessel's love for his country without exactly explaining what that country meant to him, what he saw as being at stake in the fall and occupation of France. Kessel's Russian-Jewish heritage affords another way to approach this question. Kessel's parents, both Jewish, migrated to France from Russia, each independently, in search of civil freedoms, civil rights they did not possess in Russia. And they found those freedoms in France. Kessel's father had come from an orthodox family & been intended by his mother for the Rabbinate, though his secular interests lead him not only away from religious vocation but also away from his homeland altogether. Kessel's mother had come from an area in southern Russia that had been deeply scarred by a series of increasingly brutal pogroms in the 1880s. Her own ambition had been to pursue a career in the theater, but that ambition had been crushed by Russian race laws and by the anti-Semitism of the theatrical community in Moscow. She too found refuge & freedom in France. Other members of the larger Russian community in exile, some Jewish, many others not, also fled to France from Russia following the Russian Revolution & the bloody civil war that followed it. These migrants too fled persecution and found freedom in France. And yet French society itself was — & remains — far from settled in regard to the presence of Jewish and other minority populations in its midst. Kessel's parents arrived in France just prior to the Dreyfus Affair. In that light it is unsurprising that they might have initially welcomed the opportunity to help found a Jewish community in Argentina or have returned to Russia for several crucial years during Kessel's youth. Those options were effectively the same options Kessel himself contemplated decades later when he considered his own French identity during World War Two.

Ultimately, just as his parents returned to France, Kessel too returned to France, where, despite moments of regression, the *Déclaration des droits de l'homme et du citoyen* framed a modern, secular model of community. The test for that community, as for any community, would come with the measure of diversity it could safely contain before splintering apart. World War Two posed that test in a new way.

The terms of the armistice signed with Germany by the French General & World War One hero, Marshal Philippe Pétain in June 1940 established two zones in France, one, in the North and along the Atlantic coast, occupied by the Germans, and the other, in the South, administrated by a new French government, headed by Pétain and known by the name of the spa town that would soon become its capital city, Vichy. A third portion of former French territory, in the Southeast and along the Côte d'Azur, was occupied by Italy. These administrative divisions would last until the fall of 1942, when the Allied invasion of North Africa and their struggles on the Eastern Front, provoked the Nazis to break the armistice and occupy all of France in preparation for the inevitable Allied invasion of mainland Europe.

But these are geographical & administrative facts rather than psychological ones. Psychologically speaking, the trauma of the capitulation, armistice, and not only accommodation, but also in too many cases collaboration, upon the French psyche would resonate for years to come. As Kessel put it, "the era of collaboration, of submission, of humiliation began. ... I lived more than two years in that twilight of thought, of freedom, of honor, wherein only one true flame burned: Resistance."[12] Kessel's retrospective evocation of the guiding light of resistance amidst the profound darkness & indignity of defeat hardly does justice to the shifting, uneven, and uncertain — though certainly traumatic — psychological landscape of that period in French history. Even applying the adjective French may be misleading, since France itself, the idea and therefore identity of France itself, whether understood geographically, politically, sociologically, or, more profoundly, psychologically, had been put in suspense. Capitulation put patriotism itself in question. If participation in and identification with a political entity is essential to the psychological health of human beings, as Aristotle believed, the collapse of that entity, as in that of France during World War Two, could only be experienced as profoundly traumatic to its citizens. During the armistice and occupation, the French lived a curious form of statelessness: they experienced their state as the enemy, even as its contours became distorted and all but formless under the boots of their oppressors, whether those of the Nazis or of their neighbors.

At least initially, many French men and women believed, or wanted to believe, that Marshal Pétain, the hero of Verdun, would eventually lead them, if not back to the battlefield, then perhaps into some other form of combat — political or otherwise — that would restore the nation both in terms of its territory & its dignity. Pétain was seen by many —

at least in the early days of the occupation — as a protector, if not savior, even as the relationship of France to the other nations of the world came into question. In the more or less immediate wake of the armistice, Great Britain presented the French naval commanders in North Africa, where the majority of the French fleet was harbored, with an ultimatum to either sail their fleet to Britain, or some other location outside of German hands, or be sunk. The French naval command claimed that they could be taken at their word and trusted not to collaborate with the Germans. That did not satisfy the British, who made good on their ultimatum and, through a devastating combined air & sea attack, destroyed a substantial portion of the French fleet in Mers el-Kébir, outside Oran on the Algerian coast on July 3, 1940. 1,300 French sailors lost their lives and Pétain's nascent government, scarred by this second indignity, found itself at war with England.

Given this political, social, & psychological turbulence, it is unsurprising that the period of the occupation — from late June 1940 to August 1944, from the armistice to the liberation of Paris — was far from uniform. Nor did resistance as we tend to think of it retrospectively spring up either immediately or fully formed. Even now, more than seventy years later, much about the army of shadows chronicled in Kessel's book remains in shadow. Historians like Laurent Douzou, Robert Gildea, Guillaume Piketty, and Olivier Wievorka, among many others, have recently done a tremendous amount of work to bring the details of the period, in its many shades of nuance, to light. To even speak of the occupation as a single *period*, is perhaps misguided. Moreover, and even more importantly, as Robert Gildea argues in his book, *Fighters in the Shadows: A New History of the French Resistance* (2015): "It may be more accurate to talk less about the *French* Resistance than about resistance in France."[13]

Throughout the distinct periods of the occupation, many types of people practiced many types of resistance. Indeed, each period of the occupation called for the creation of new types of resistance, & that is also to say new types of resistors, willing to undertake new types of anti-Nazi activities. The propaganda and information war waged in underground newspapers & books was, for example, different from the war of rescue and escape waged in visa & passport offices and in hidden rooms and basements in small towns and villages. A bureaucrat forging a visa was nevertheless also quite different from a resistor willing to undertake industrial or military sabotage. Similarly, asking someone to blow up a train or factory under cover of night was quite different from asking someone to kill an enemy combatant — whether German or collaborationist, military or civilian — in cold blood. Each of these types of resistance resulted from, demanded, and fulfilled a motivating social & political vision, an understanding of the ideas or outrages that might be worth a fight and not just a fight, but murder. Those competing and highly personal political visions were by turns traditional, nascent, and so newly founded as to be amorphous, unstable, and in some cases, unconvincing, even ultimately untenable. It is one thing to ask an individual to enlist in an army sanctioned

by the state, to willingly and knowingly become outfitted &
trained as a soldier on behalf of a legitimate and therefore legitimating nation at the outbreak of a war. It is quite another
to ask that same individual to conjure that sanction on his
own, from the depths of his soul, in the darkness of indignity.
The transformation of a civil engineer, for example, into an
assassin, however civically minded, is, in short, no easy thing.
It betrays a psychological convulsion in the life of a man, & in
this case, on this scale, in the soul of a nation. *Army of Shadows* stands witness to just such a convulsion. And it does not
stand alone. The roots of resistance, the process of transform-
ing everyday people into an army of shadows, would haunt
France, as it would any nation. In 1951, six years after the end
of the war, Albert Camus wrote his book *The Rebel* in an attempt to address the enigma posed by the transformation. As
he put it, "We shall know nothing until we know whether we
have the right to kill our fellow men, or the right to let them
be killed. In that every action today leads to murder, direct
or indirect, we cannot act until we know whether or why we
have the right to kill." [14]

Robert Gildea outlines the competing political visions
motivating resistance in France succinctly. In discussing the
exploits of Gilbert Renault, who is perhaps better known by
his code name, Colonel Rémy, Gildea writes about the

> tension between the Free French, who thought that
> the purpose of resistance was basically to facilitate
> military activity to liberate France and Europe, and

metropolitan resistors, who realized that the old world had been discredited or destroyed and that resistance involved a political rethinking of how France and even Europe would have to be reconstructed after liberation. This clash of visions had profound implications for the conduct of the Resistance: would it be the secret underground conspiracy of a few in collaboration with the Allies or would it be a more popular movement of French people who wished to take matters into their own hands and remake their futures?[15]

The political visions motivating resistance in France were, in short, multiple, competitive, and at times contradictory. Some were retrospective — rooted in a traditional, often even Catholic vision of France — while others were prospective, proposed as a part of a process of reimagining social relations in France, Europe, & the world. Nor was the resistance itself a unified or homogenous social body. As the recent histories of the resistance movements have shown, there was not *one* resistance but many, drawn from many social groups within France and in fact internationally. A great many Spanish Republicans who fought fascism in Spain during the Spanish Civil War from 1936 to 1939 retreated across the Pyrenees into France at the end of that conflict. With the Nazi occupation of France, they were prepared — & trained, disciplined — to take up arms against a Fascist oppressor. Many Italian anti-fascists too had come across the border between France and Italy since Mussolini came to power there in the early 1920s. Like the Spanish Republicans, they were an organized anti-fascist force prepared to engage in resistance activities. Other displaced and refugee populations were also among those inclined to fight. Many Poles and others from Eastern Europe and elsewhere had migrated to France between the wars in search of work in a heavily industrialized nation whose working age male population had been decimated by the First World War. When Germany invaded Poland in September 1939, Poles living in France were cut off from their ancestral home and motivated to fight for it from afar. Some German anti-fascists too had sought refuge in France as the Nazis tightened their grip on Germany in the 1930s. Under conditions of occupation, unable to run, they would stand and fight. Each of those groups came to the fight with different motivations, different goals, and, significantly, different levels of training, discipline, & general preparedness.

Among those many groups, the communists stood apart. At that time in Europe, communism was an active political philosophy and social movement, a dream that had then only recently become a kind of reality in Soviet Russia but that also promised — or threatened — to become one elsewhere, indeed almost everywhere. The communists were organized, disciplined, and politically sophisticated. They understood the value of propaganda and knew how to create and disseminate underground publications. But they also understood the difference between a war of words and a war. For many communists, anti-fascist resistance was only another part of what they believed would ultimately be a worldwide revolution. This view benefitted them in carrying out their resistance activities, even as it occasionally forbid their collaboration with other resistance networks. During the period of the German pact with the Soviet Union, from 1939 until the German invasion of Russia in the summer of 1941, even after the invasion and occupation of France in 1940, many communists in France obeyed orders from Moscow not to violate the Soviet pact with Germany by engaging in resistance activity of any kind. Thus the first year of the occupation saw the members of the most disciplined underground network in France — that of the communists — sidelined, sitting on their hands. That situation would change — instantly and radically — with the invasion of Russia but it provides a profound example of the power of political vision in motivating resistance activity. The communists in France would ultimately be crucial partners in the resistance even though their international political vision conflicted profoundly with the national vision of the Free French and other groups. Kessel paid the communists significant and due respect in *Army of Shadows*, in the words of Philippe Gerbier: "I don't know of a man in the resistance who does not speak of the communists with a special quality in his voice & face. A deeper gravity." Or again:

> The Communists are the masters of such divisions
> [between groups], as everything in the underground
> life. Mathilde returns marveling at the strength, dis-
> cipline, and method that she encounters in their

> homes. But short of making underground action for
> a quarter century, we cannot match them. They are
> professionals; we're still paying our dues.

This distinction between the communists and others in the resistance brings to mind Jean Améry's moving remarks on the value of political & religious faith in grounding activism. Améry was himself tortured and deported to Auschwitz after having engaged in minor political activism (distributing pamphlets). Reflecting on his experience as an intellectual and agnostic in the camps alongside politically & religiously motivated prisoners, he admitted: "One way or the other, in the decisive moments their political or religious belief was an inestimable help to them, while we skeptical and humanistic intellectuals took recourse, in vain, to our literary, philosophical, & artistic household gods. Whether they were militant Marxists, sectarian Jehovah's Witnesses, or practicing Catholics, whether they were highly educated national economists and theologians or less versed workers & peasants, their belief or their ideology gave them the firm foothold in the world from which they spiritually unhinged the SS state."[16] Lacking such a foothold, one felt adrift, amorphous, uncertain, wracked by questions of purpose, sanction, and legitimacy.

Jews were another group that stood apart in the resistance. Some Jews in France were of German, Polish, or Eastern European descent and had only recently relocated to France, along with many others between the wars. A great many came during the late 1930s as the Nazis tightened their race laws, more than doubling the population of Jews in France within a few short years. The situation became acute after 1939, when both Britain and the United States closed their borders to additional Jewish refugees. During the occupation, the Vichy government promulgated discriminatory race laws similar to those of Germany. Jews in occupied France would ultimately be arrested and held in camps in both occupied France and Vichy. Beginning in the spring of 1942, Jews in France began to be deported to Auschwitz. This both motivated Jewish participation in resistance activities and increased the stakes of that participation. Moreover, under conditions of generalized anti-Semitism, Jewish participation in resistance activities was itself a challenge. Not every network welcomed the participation of Jews. In Kessel's *Army of Shadows*, unsurprisingly, given his emanci-pated, secular perspective, Jews were welcome & esteemed: "When a man of the resistance is taken on mere suspicion, he still has some chance of surviving, but if this man is a Jew, he is sure to die in the most atrocious way. Despite this there are many Jews in our organizations." The text is quite clear about the fate of Jews deported to the East. As Gerbier listens to the tales of his fellow prisoners prior to his run through the shooting range, he hears the story of a rabbi assigned to a committee whose purpose was to identify Jews in France. Those Jews that the rabbi identified were to be deported to Poland "to die." When the rabbi failed to cooperate, he was himself condemned to death.

The presence of women in Kessel's *Army of Shadows* is worthy of similar note. As Gildea and others have shown, at the beginning of the occupation, many French men of military age were either in POW camps or otherwise dispersed. The responsibility of resistance thus fell, at least initially, to women and older men.[17] Kessel shows his readers this reality through the characters of Mathilde and Augustine Viellat, among others. The wives and daughters of resistors also joined the fight. Though this fact would be overlooked by a generation of historians, Kessel was acutely sensitive to the reality of it, not least because his mistress of many years, Germaine Sablon, was active within the same resistance network as he was in the southern zone in 1941 & 1942.

Kessel's own participation in resistance activities during those years undoubtedly helped him ground the text in reality, even though it does nothing to account for the almost astonishing variety of details and the volume and range of stories and events recounted in *Army of Shadows*. Following his decommission in the fall of 1940, Kessel went south, to work as a reporter for *Paris-Soir* in Marseille. Germaine Sablon was already living in the southern zone. That first year of the occupation saw Kessel searching his soul in the way that writers often do, namely, by writing. Alongside his journalism, he wrote a short novel about a pilot who decides to join the then still nascent resistance. The book, *Les Maudru* (The Maudru, 1945), lacks the richness of physical and psychological detail found in *Army of Shadows*, and reads as a somewhat stereotypical sketch of the circumstances in which it was written, as if Kessel were simply pushing stock characters and situations around in his mind, ruminating in the workman-like prose of a thriller. The subject matter was nevertheless politically incendiary, and therefore impossible to publish, certainly from the pen of a writer whose books had already been banned. Kessel literally buried the manuscript, but, more importantly, he also followed in the footsteps of his characters shortly thereafter, by joining the resistance himself.

When approached by Emmanuel d'Astier de la Vigerie from the Libération network, Kessel turned away, fearing that the group was too undisciplined. Ultimately he joined the Carte resistance network directed by André Girard.[18] Throughout 1941 and 1942, and despite his renown, operating under the name Joseph Pascal, he delivered information and guns, & helped stage embarkations to England like the ones described in *Army of Shadows*.[19] In November 1942, as the occupying forces redoubled their search for Jews in France — including among their list of names, Joseph and Georges Kessel — the Allies landed in Morocco and Algeria and the German army flooded into the southern zone. By the end of the month, the Carte network would be burned, Kessel's cover blown. By then it would also be too dangerous for Lysanders, the light aircraft used by the R.A.F. to support the resistance, to land, and too risky for embarkations by sea as well. Kessel, Germaine, & Maurice Druon, Kessel's nephew who was also part of the network, were left with few options. The one they chose led them over the Pyrenees under cover of darkness with a small group of other refugees, into and ultimately across Spain, to neutral Portugal where they could obtain passage from Lisbon to London by the beginning of the new year.

Kessel spent his first month in England cooling his heels at a manor house in the countryside known as the Patriotic School, essentially a holding pen and interrogation center for anyone who had recently come from the continent under even potentially suspicious circumstances. The fact that Kessel was one of the most famous writers in France, whose name, photograph, and anti-fascist views were well known from the front pages of newspapers, gave the process the ironic air of comedy. He recalled the incident many years later with his usual élan:

> Undoubtedly I had published journalism against Hitler in the most renowned French dailies, undoubtedly I had taken the side of the Republicans in Spain during the civil war, undoubtedly I had been part of a resistance network linked to London. But that proved nothing. Nothing.[20]

His interrogator was well aware of Kessel's life and position but nevertheless went through the process of verification required of them both. By the end of January, Kessel had been cleared and was at his liberty to join the Free French.

After nearly two months of travel and interrogation, Kessel arrived in London on January 23, 1943. For Charles de Gaulle, the leader of the Free French Forces, the timing could not have been better. At the end of November 1942, the celebrated pilot and author, and Kessel's friend, Antoine de Saint-Exupéry, who had been living in New York since December 1940, had published an "Open Letter to Frenchmen Everywhere," first in the *New York Times Magazine* and shortly thereafter in newspapers in Canada & North Africa, in which he argued for a vision of France set above political parties, thereby both accepting of Pétain's role in the capitulation and also implicitly critical of de Gaulle's attempts to lead solely on his own terms.[21] Saint-Exupéry even advocated incorporating exiled French forces into the United States or some other existing military structure "outside politics".[22] For de Gaulle, who had established himself as the leader of the Free French from his base in London, and whose voice broadcast to France by the BBC was, for many, the voice of the Free French, even the voice of France itself, this view was utterly unacceptable. The depth of de Gaulle's concern over these views can only be understood in light of his tenuous hold on power. The Germans, for their part, recognized Marshal Pétain as the legitimate leader of the French: Pétain signed the armistice & was the head of the government in Vichy. Even then, in late 1942, these facts held sway over some portion of the French population and, worse, the rest of the world. Still worse for de Gaulle, the American government — which had entered the war in December 1941 — did not fully believe in him, in his ability to unify and lead the French toward a democratic — rather than dictatorial — future. While Winston Churchill and the British government backed de Gaulle and supported him in London, the Americans went looking for their own French military hero to back in a bid to lead the French forces &, ultimately, government. They found such a figure in General Henri Giraud, who had escaped German captivity and was then living quietly in the south of France. By backing Giraud, the Americans created a three-way power struggle for both real and symbolic leadership of the French nation.

All of this in mind, it is hardly surprising that de Gaulle agreed to meet Joseph Kessel at his headquarters in Carlton Gardens soon after Kessel's release from the Patriotic School. The General needed the writer's help. The meeting nevertheless made an enormous impression upon Kessel. When he asked de Gaulle about the war, about how it would end, de Gaulle replied, with absolute confidence and sincerity, "My dear, it's finished, it's won. There are only a few formalities to fulfill." [23] While we might retrospectively agree with the General's assessment — the battle for Stalingrad had just ended, marking perhaps the decisive turning point in the war — the statement still signals a significant and significantly compelling vision on the behalf of de Gaulle as a leader. The two men spoke of Kessel's recent experiences in the resistance as well as of his background in the military. Though he was at the time in his mid-forties, Kessel wanted to get back into the fight, preferably in some capacity related to aviation. But de Gaulle quickly and unsurprisingly dashed his hopes, asking him instead to travel to the United States & promote the Free French cause there through journalism and other propaganda. Kessel however didn't want to leave England, to be so far from his family in occupied France. De Gaulle proposed a compromise: stay in England and write a book about the resistance. Kessel agreed. The book he wrote was *Army of Shadows*.[24]

Kessel set to work, though not initially on the novel. First, he reconnected with Charles Gombault, an old friend from the newspaper *Paris-Soir*, now living in exile in London and publishing a new paper, *France*. Gombault enthusiastically agreed to publish whatever Kessel might want to bring to print in the coming months. *France* and other publications, including papers based in newly liberated French North Africa, would provide venues for Kessel to continue his resistance activities in a war of words. "How Marshal Pétain Died," an implacable attack on the Vichy leader, fatally eroding his image, was among his first articles. Other articles looked back at the events Kessel had witnessed over the previous two years in France.[25] Many of these pieces would be translated into English and published in London and elsewhere, in papers like the *Evening Standard* and the *Daily Express*.

From March 1943 through late 1944, Kessel published articles and other pieces, some of which would ultimately be draft chapters of *Army of Shadows* in several different newspapers and journals, each of which had a distinct political slant, either in favor of or in some cases violently opposed to Charles de Gaulle as the presumptive leader of the Free French. *La Marseilleaise* (Algiers) was a Gaullist paper, but

France (London) and *France-Libre* (London) were each at least initially anti-Gaullist, *France-Libre* violently so. Charles Gombault, Kessel's friend from *Paris-Soir*, would however soon temper his paper's criticism of de Gaulle in keeping with Kessel's own politics of friendship. André Labarthe & Raymond Aron published *France-Libre*. Kessel also published in *L'Arche* (Algiers), *Pour la Victoire* (New York), *La Marseillaise* (Cairo), *France-Amérique* (New York), and *Fontaine* (Algiers), among other papers, all of which fell somewhere on the even then contentious Gaullist / anti-Gaullist spectrum. Anne Simonin situates Kessel in this mix as being the "most ecumenical" Gaullist. [26]

In the midst of this activity, in May 1943, Kessel and his nephew, Maurice Druon, who had long since also been released from Patriotic School, wrote lyrics in French to the melody of a Russian-Jewish song of resistance sung by another Russian exile, Anna Marly. They gave it the title *Chant des partisans* (Song of the Partisans). Kessel's mistress, Germaine Sablon, recorded the song for the first time at the end of the month. Broadcast to France by the BBC, the song spread rapidly throughout the country & around the world & quickly became the unofficial anthem of the resistance. It was undoubtedly the single most important act of æsthetic or artistic resistance of the World War Two era.

Kessel meanwhile continued to work on the book he had promised de Gaulle. His own experience in the Carte network provided a useful starting point for the project. He could rely on his own memories & on the testimony of some of the people who had been active in the network alongside him. On March 7, 1943, he published a preliminary gathering of some testimony about the resistance in the southern zone under the title, "Le visage de la grande espérance" (The Face of the Great Hope).[27] But he needed more information as well and, somewhat ironically, he had better access to it in London than he did in occupied France, where secrecy was key to survival. In the version of the preface included in the first English language editions of the book, Kessel explained:

> It was my good fortune to have in France as friends men like Gerbier, Lemasque, or Felix la Tonsure. But it was in London that I was able to see the French Resistance in its most vivid light. This is not so surprising as it may seem. For the obligation of secrecy, the fact of being hunted quarry, made all encounters on the native soil difficult and precarious. In London one can meet and talk freely. In London all the surviving leaders of the Resistance turn up sooner or later. And this extraordinary coming-and-going between France and England appears quite natural here. London is the crossroads of the strangest destines of France.

In *L'Heure des Châtiments* (The Hour of Punishment), Kessel was even more explicit:

> In France, I spent more than two years in contact of all kinds with the Resistance: clandestine newspapers, intelligence networks, action groups, elements

of the secret army. It was in London, however — *&*
in a few weeks — that I discovered the true breadth
and depth of the underground struggle, and of its
countless aspects, and its marvelous faces. The
paradox was only apparent. It was in fact in London where the documents arrived that sent the men
out. It was from London that the orders, the armies,
the secret agents departed. There one had an overall
view of the clandestine struggle. One followed, from
day to day, the successes and torments, through the
broadcasts of mysterious radios, through the reports
that came across the sealed borders. [28]

The book quite simply could not have been written in
France during the occupation. In London, Kessel interviewed
members of the resistance as they passed through the Free
French headquarters in between clandestine missions. Once
again his skill as a journalist served his novelistic imagination.
For this reason he could write, at the beginning of the preface:

There is no propaganda in this book and there is no
fiction. No detail has been forced, and none have
been invented. You will find assembled here, without formality and sometimes even randomly, only
authentic, proven, verified, and thus commonplace
facts. The current events of French life. The sources
are numerous and trustworthy.

The characters and events are rooted in reality. It is a non-
fiction novel or what might later be termed true fiction.[29]

However, the book bears a double necessity, that of secrecy alongside that of testimony. If Kessel's characters resembled their real life counterparts too closely, they might endanger those individuals who served as their models as well as the lives of members of their families or networks. With this in mind, Kessel changed details, locations, key elements, creating "composite sketches" of individuals rather than distinctly recognizable representations of real people. Details were recast, relocated, all but utterly reimagined, toward a new version of the reality upon which they had been based. Some characters took on the deeds of a great many others. The names too have of course been changed. This despite the fact that the names of resistance fighters were already false names, giving the text a nested dolls or hall of mirrors effect: lies within lies on parade toward the truth.

Some of the real life models are nevertheless visible to us now, behind the distorted and composite, fictional masks. The deeds and character of Mathilde bear recognized resemblance to those of at least three known resisters: Lucie Aubrac, Dominique Desanti, & Maude Begon. Saint Luc is said to have been based on the resistance hero Jean Moulin, though he also bears comparison with Emmanuel d'Astier and others. The real life communist deputy who escaped from Châteaubriant was named Fernand Gernier. He made his escape on June 19, 1941, and went on to represent the Communist Party in London after his arrival there in January 1943. Philippe Gerbier brings together several well-known figures as well. These include Gilbert Védy, known in the resistance as Jacques Médéric, Gilbert Renault, known as Colonel Rémy, & Jean Gosset. [30]

All of this in mind, simply reading the book as a kind of *réportage à clef*, attempting to decode the key, to link the characters with real-life counterparts, misses at least one central point of the book: namely that Kessel's characters are not necessarily meant to be singular or anomalous individuals but rather stand-ins for a cast of thousands. The events aren't singular; they are symptomatic. The details ground them in a visceral & moving reality that is nevertheless interchangeable with myriad others. A thousand other stories could have been inserted in their place. In this way, the book is perhaps in some ways closest to myth, a myth of resistance in France. And at this point, as in Greek tragic theater, the audience already knows the story.

Also as in myth, the strict chronology of the events is secondary. The chapters are in fact occasionally only loosely affiliated in time. Sometimes the narrative is quite close to the events recounted, observing them in great detail, intimately. In other sections, tracks of time pass without remark, leaving the reader to wonder whether days passed or months. Nevertheless, the book is firmly rooted in time & space. Many details suggest the precise moment in the story of France and the story of resistance when the events take place. France, for example, is still divided into two zones. When the wife on the farm, Augustine, says that she hopes British soldiers are welcome in all good French homes, she is reflecting a sentiment that was relatively uncommon during the first period of the occupation, just after the British sank a large part of the French navy in North Africa. There are references to the beginning of deportations to the East, including of Jews to Poland. Though Jews were rounded up and placed in camps in occupied France, particularly beginning in 1941, the actual deportations did not begin until March 27, 1942. The Renault factory bombing mentioned in the text also occurred during March of 1942: it was however done by the British Royal Air Force rather than by the American Air Force, as Kessel claims, perhaps disingenuously. The book is thus both rooted in a very specific moment in the war — 1942, prior to the end of the Armistice — & all but timeless.

The book is also at once highly stylized, written with subtle attention to nuances of literary strategy, and very loosely structured, almost collage-like in form. As Gerbier introduces Legrain to the details of the resistance, for example, Kessel is also subtly introducing his reader to those details as well: allowing us — the readers — to share Legrain's astonishment, his chagrin, his fear, and his hopefulness, to feel that we too are reading this under conditions of occupation, that we too might be moved to join in the fight. Other scenes deploy strategies and effects that recall those of scenes from other books by Kessel. The execution of the traitor early in the book, for example, recalls in some ways Kessel's short story "Le Caveau № 7" (Cave 7) from *Mémoires d'un Commissaire du Peuple* (Memoirs of a Commissioner of the People, 1925), a collection of stories Kessel wrote about Russia after the October Revolution, in which an executioner is too close to the victim of an execution and the deed itself challenged by the physical details, the very flesh of the victim.

But *Army of Shadows* is also very loosely structured as well. The third chapter focuses on a character that had not yet appeared up until that point, Jean-François. In the fourth chapter, a first-person narrator appears in a narrative that had previously been recounted only in the third person. The fifth chapter presents a collage of brief sketches, some as short as a sentence, others as long as a few paragraphs. These "notes" are recounted in the first person, though the character has shifted from the previous chapter, now we are reading the thoughts of the main character, Philippe Gerbier. The book as a whole is thus a kaleidoscope and a collage built of multiple perspectives, both abstract & intimate, of its subject matter.

The "notes" of Philippe Gerbier also offer us a metatextual comment on the book itself. The voice of Gerbier tells us:

> Subjective opinions & feelings have no value. The truth is only in facts. I want, when I am free, to keep a record of the facts that may affect a man whom events have put at a good observation point to the resistance. Much later, with hindsight, these accumulated details will in sum allow me to form a judgment. If I survive.

Kessel's multiplication of perspectives helps erode the "subjectivity" of the text, pushing it toward a more objective point of view, while still framing the meaning of the events in human concern. Ultimately, as a novel, the book withholds the judgment Gerbier promises, leaving it up to the reader to reach his or her own conclusions. Some of the possible conclusions may however be surprising in a book intended as a celebration of national heroism.

Already in the preface, Kessel announces the fundamental psychological challenge of the book. Under conditions of occupation, as Kessel observes: "France no longer has bread, wine, fire. But mainly it no longer has any laws. Civil disobedience, individual or organized rebellion, have become duties to the fatherland. The national hero is the clandestine man, the outlaw." Later on, in "Philippe Gerbier's Notes," he goes further: "The laws, rules, no longer exist." The situation was one of terrible paradox. How can civil disobedience be an obligation in the absence of recognized law? How can the national hero be an *outlaw* in the absence of *law*? Civil disobedience in fact depends upon the existence of the state and the idea of the law. Though disobedient, dissent is still civil. As Hannah Arendt has argued, dissent rests upon a tacit civil consent.[31] In the absence of recognized civil authority, in the absence of the law, dissent itself is both formless & groundless or, more accurately, must assert itself from a groundless, baseless position. Whether that position is conceived of as being alongside, before, or beyond the law, it is baseless, rootless; sanctioned or justified by no authority, limited by no logic, shaped by no formal structures. Indeed, a recognized, functionally viable state provides both the internal structure and the outer bounds of the political entity. The internal structure defines stable & valid mechanisms of participation in civil life, including forms of dissent, both legal & illegal. The outer circumference determines the space within which politics of any kind — from peaceful democracy to the stasis of civil conflict — can take place. In the absence of that outer limit, no center can hold. This is the chasm of politics, the erosion of the state from both within & without.

Moreover, as Kessel demonstrates, the chasm of politics is as much a psychological condition as it is a sociological or political one. The ability to act — including acts of resistance — is dependent upon our confidence in at least tacit assumptions about individual and social life. Acknowledging, as Kessel does, what Arendt later described as the "criminalization of the whole governmental apparatus,"[32] those fundamental political and social assumptions are revealed to be groundless: and one is uprooted, cast adrift, easy prey to terror and paralysis. At the other extreme, however, such circumstances might also occasion and be unable to contain a boundless explosion of the id, of thanatos. In the absence of the law, everything is permitted.

From the relatively safe distance of the immediate aftermath of the war, Jean-Paul Sartre eulogized the conditions of occupation as those of ultimate freedom:

> Never were we freer than under the German Occupation ... The often atrocious circumstances of our struggle made it possible, in a word, for us to live out that unbearable, heart-rending situation known as the human condition in a candid, unvarnished way.[33]

But read in light of *Army of Shadows*, the easy confidence of Sartre's postwar polemic is revealed as shallow, indeed as being too easy. Yes, the political revelation of the occupation — the daily confrontation with one's enemies, the collapse of the supportive logic and justification of the legitimate state — might reveal one's fundamental freedom in an unvarnished way, but such revelations are not liberating, they are tragic.

In July 1943, while Kessel was writing *Army of Shadows*, Albert Camus published the first of his *Letters to a German Friend* in the clandestine paper, *Revue Libre*. Closer than Sartre to Kessel's position, Camus observed:

> It is not much to be able to do violence when you have been simply preparing for it for years and when violence is more natural to you than thinking. It is a great deal, on the other hand, to face torture and death when you know for a fact that hatred and violence are empty things in themselves. It is a great deal to fight while despising war, to accept losing everything while still preferring happiness, to face destruction while cherishing the idea of a higher civilization. That is how we do more than you, because we have to draw on ourselves. You [Germans] had nothing to conquer in your heart or in your intelligence. We had two enemies, and a military victory was not enough for us, as it was for you who had nothing to overcome.[34]

The self-overcoming of the French, their internal struggle to strangle within themselves their respect for human rights and love of peace, their willingness to extend the hand of friendship, as Camus says elsewhere in the letter, rather than violent blows, was neither easy nor immediate. *Army of Shadows* is, in many ways, the story of this self-overcoming; the story of a fundamental change in the character and consciousness of the French under the conditions of occupation.

In the novel, after watching a postman & a saddle maker assassinate two S.S. officers, Félix flatly remarks: "They've certainly changed, the French." "Philippe Gerbier's Notes" include a more thorough & brutal assessment of the change:

> The French were not prepared, not disposed to kill. Their temperament, their climate, their country, the state of civilization they had reached, warded them off bloodshed. I remember how, in the early days of the resistance, it was difficult to envisage cold-blooded murder, ambushes, planned assassinations. And how it was difficult to recruit people for this. There is no question now of such repugnance! Primitive man has reappeared in the French. They kill to defend their home, their bread, their loves, their honor. They kill every day. They kill the German, the traitor, the informer. They kill for a reason and they kill by reflex. I will not say that the French people have hardened. They have grown sharper.

This transformation is not only presented in the abstract. It's there in the lives of almost all of the main characters, though not always in such a linear fashion. Again in "Philippe Gerbier's Notes," we encounter Gerbier's reflection about the changes undergone by those who join the resistance:

> I believe that among the people of the resistance, an evolution is in process where they develop the inverse aspect of their temperaments. Those who were sweet, tender, peaceful, they become hard. Those who were as hard as I was, as I still am, become more permeable to feelings.

Nor are the changes all or always described as being negative. Again from "Philippe Gerbier's Notes," recounting the story of a resistor Gerbier encountered in London: "I well know that that gesture was stupid, my companion then told me, but I haven't been in France for three years. The discovery of this new people makes my head turn a bit." Some of the characters, including Gerbier, allude with occasional astonishment to their previous lives, in his case as an engineer. Others, like Jean-François, Lemasque, or Mathilde, join the resistance in the course of the book and change with it. In other cases, characters are equally astonished by the recognition of changes — or perhaps the revelation of heretofore unsurfaced capacities of others, as in the case of Jean-François when he learned the identity of the leader of their network. Part of this is to say that the disconcerting element of the changes wrought by the necessity of resistance upon the soul of the French is not confined to the capacity for violence unleashed, but rather extends more deeply to the more fundamental malleability of humankind. The revelation of the range of possibility within an individual, alongside the malleability of that individual, is deeply unsettling both to others and to that individual. All of this in mind, it is fair to say that *Army of Shadows* is as much about amorphousness and change as it is about fidelity to the cause of resistance. The army of shadows is an army *in* the shadows, but it is also an army *of* shadows, of shadow men and women who become shades of themselves: inconstant, insubstantial, changeable figures.

Many of the characters confront this fundamental fact of their humanity either directly or indirectly in the text. They encounter their own limits as agents of resistance and as human beings. When thinking about the leader, Jean-François reflects: "If he was like me, he wouldn't be the big boss." Everyone has their own capacities, their own part to play, but also their own limits. In perhaps the most extreme extrapolation of this theme in the book, when Gerbier realizes that he is about to die, he does not recognize the inner voice that brings this recognition. In confronting his own death, he becomes a stranger to himself. Later, after his rescue, when admitting this moment of weakness with the leader of his network, Luc Jardie, Jardie laughs, "I don't think it's lamentable to be a man," he says, suggesting that to be human is to be frail, changeable: capable of losing confidence in oneself & faith in one's ideals.

Significantly, Luc Jardie, the leader of the resistance network chronicled in the book, never waivers. Gerbier observes: "The boss alone still remains true to himself. I think that he has long since accepted the possibilities of good and evil which each human being unconsciously carries within himself." Gerbier's — & by extension Kessel's — faith in such a figure is a key to the Gaullism of the text. Jardie alone is steadfast, certain, & unwavering. Though based on other historical figures as well, his character is certainly also a stand-in for Charles de Gaulle himself. Jardie stands as the final authority and ultimate arbiter in every decision, amid the chaos of the lawless land, he is recognized as a legitimate and therefore also legitimating authority. Even more, in prison, condemned to death, Gerbier realizes that love for him means love & respect for his leader, who he calls Saint Luc. "Saint Luc is whom I love most in life, but Saint Luc could disappear and I would still like to live." Even Saint Luc is a stand-in for another, higher authority. Twenty-years later, in 1964, reflecting similar sentiments during a ceremony commemorating the transfer of the remains of resistance hero Jean Moulin to the Panthéon, André Malraux, then Minister of Culture, eulogized Moulin, but also de Gaulle, who was then President of the Republic. Malraux said of de Gaulle: he "alone could summon the Resistance movements to union among themselves and with all the other combats, for only through him did France wage a single combat."[35] Such was the spirit of Gaullism among its committed adherents.

Despite the singularity of this love, the emerging myth of the resistance proposed the resistance itself as *the* essential political community of France. If *Army of Shadows* began with an evocation of the lawlessness and dissolution of the state, with the recognition that states too decompose, the book ultimately observed that the meaning of France had shifted, put bluntly in the book: "Today the Republic is in the maquis." This shift was not an easy one &, in 1942-43, it was far from certain or even necessarily widespread. As noted above, the maquis, the resistance itself was far from unified. Nevertheless, as the character Jean-François observes in *Army of Shadows* — with what would later be revealed as deep irony — he felt closer to his comrades in the resistance than to his own brother. "Now he had to hide everything, except from his companions of the secret war. And this made them, for Jean-François, his true people." This is an assertion of community but also a denial of one. The occupation and attendant resistance created a new kind of clandestine community in France, a new civic bond that was of necessity both hidden and silent. In the essay quoted above, Jean-Paul Sartre concurred with this sentiment: "In the shadows and in blood, the strongest of Republics was forged."[36] Sartre and many others hoped that the spirit & community of the resistance would carry on into the postwar period. Needless to say, those hopes would not be fulfilled, not least because, however compelling, they were all but utterly mythical imaginary projections, legends, at their point of origin.

Joseph Kessel wrote *Army of Shadows* as a concrete act of resistance, of war by other means. He did so at the personal request of Charles de Gaulle, but also to serve as moral and political motivation for many other readers as well: for the French community in exile, in London and New York, and for those, particularly among the English and Americans, who might be in a position to help the French. Kessel took care to mask the identities of his characters even though the direct distribution of the book in occupied France was difficult if not impossible. In his efforts to disseminate the work, Kessel also published all but one of the chapters, often with variations, in French language newspapers and journals in London, New York, Algiers, and Cairo, during the months surrounding the publication of the book as a whole in 1943 & 1944.[37] Under wartime conditions and from his position in exile in London, Kessel could not publish the book with his normal publisher, Éditions Gallimard. Instead, the book was first published in Algiers in November 1943 by Edmund Charlot, the publisher of *France Libre*, who had also published books by André Gide, Jean Grenier, Georges Bernanos, & Albert Camus. Jacques Schiffrin released a second French language edition of the book in New York in 1944 through his newly founded press, Pantheon. Schiffrin had created the prestigious Éditions de la Pléiâde in France in 1931 but, during the first days of the occupation, as another Russian-born French Jew, he had been "purged" from Gallimard, which published the Pléiâde after 1936 & was then facing pressure from the Nazis. In New York, Schiffrin founded Pantheon

& published writings associated with the French resistance, including Vercors' *Le Silence de la Mer* (The Silence of the Sea) in 1942, poetry by Louis Aragon, and Kessel's *Army of Shadows*.[38] That same year, Haakon Chevalier translated the book into English for publication by Alfred Knopf in the United States and Cresset Press in England.[39] The preface to the English language editions of the book differs from that of the French edition: it includes passages, including some quoted above, wherein Kessel reflects upon the availability of information about the resistance in London and concludes with a signature line, dating the work to September 8, 1943 & locating it at Kessel's home there, Kinnerton Studio.[40] Since these details link the text so closely to Kessel's time in London, it is unsurprising that he would omit them from the French version of the text. After the liberation of Paris, a new French edition of *Army of Shadows* appeared in metropolitan France through the combined efforts of Charlot & Éditions Julliard in 1945. But by then the book was already part of history.

Following the Allied invasion of the Atlantic coast of France on June 6, 1944, D-Day, the war took another decisive turn, as did the activities of the Resistance along with it. The army of shadows came increasingly — if not fully — out into the open, both providing support for the Allied offensive with sabotage and also occasionally targeting the German military in its retreat. But this moment was fraught with as much tense ambiguity as overt hostility. As noted previously, the goals of the Free French — of Charles de Gaulle in particular —, the various Resistance networks, and the

Allies were profoundly distinct, even in opposition to one another. The Allies were intent on pushing the Germans back into Germany above all else and regarded the French with suspicion both militarily & politically: they had, after all, suffered a catastrophic defeat at the hands of the Nazis. The goals of the Resistance networks were also as diverse as were those groups themselves. Many Resistance leaders hoped to transform their networks into political parties in the postwar period, which was now visible on the immediate horizon, and their political ambitions impacted, in some cases, their military discipline. De Gaulle's main purpose was nevertheless to preserve the *continuity* of France as a political entity, this despite four years of Armistice under Vichy. Members of the United States government, including President Roosevelt, actively considered imposing an Allied Military Government in Occupied Territory on France as they had already done in Italy. Many communists among the Resistance hoped to establish an entirely new political structure in postwar France in alliance with the Soviets. Amid the distrust and furor, the war was still to be won. Charles de Gaulle scored a major coup when he successfully argued that the Free French Forces should be allowed to spearhead the recapture of Paris even though this was almost purely a symbolic victory, without meaningful military significance to the Allies. Thus by the last days of August 1944, de Gaulle would be in position to address the jubilant crowds in the French capital and proclaim their liberation. Almost immediately thereafter he took charge of a new Provisional Government of the French Republic which sought to bring together all of the factions tearing at the new political landscape of France while also facing the staggering challenges left by the turmoil of the war years: cities in ruin, a ravaged industrial and agricultural infrastructure, shortages of basic goods, food most importantly, a colonial empire on the verge of collapse, and of course the legacy of personal, social, and political collaboration with the Nazis during the years of occupation. Though elected as head of the government following Parliamentary elections in October 1945, de Gaulle would resign less than four months later, unable to form a stable, coherent government between all of the fractious parties. He stepped back from the front lines of French politics almost immediately, retiring to his country estate to write his war memoirs.

Joseph Kessel also moved on rather quickly following the publication of *Army of Shadows*. After a brief, "diplomatic" mission to Hollywood, exploring the possibilities of joint French and American productions linked to the war effort, Kessel got his wish to return to a more direct form of military duty, when he was appointed "acting captain" of the French volunteers in the Sussex squadron air corps. The group flew missions over France collecting information broadcast from radios on the ground. After the war he returned to his work as a journalist and writer, continuing to travel and report from crisis zones around the world, from the newly founded state of Israel, in the late 1940s, to Afghanistan in the late 1960s. In addition to the Nuremberg trials, he covered the trials of Marshal Pétain and, in 1961, Adolf Eichmann.

His greatest literary success — in both critical & financial terms — came in 1958 with the publication of a short fable, *Le Lion* (The Lion) which won the Prix des Ambassadeurs that year and would be made into a film in 1962.

The same year Kessel published *Le Lion* the profoundly unstable French government was again on the edge of collapse. Despite economic gains since the war, the humiliating retreat from Indochina in 1954 and the on-going war in Algeria, combined with the persistent, sharp divisions in the French political community, created conditions of political stasis verging insistently on civil war. As the struggle for independence in Algeria deepened, French colonial settlers, now native North Africans known as Pied-Noir, struggled to maintain their ties to France. In May 1958, Pied-Noir militants occupied government buildings in Algiers, the capital of Algeria. Almost immediately the French military took control. The rebellion verged on becoming a more generalized coup when paratroopers affiliated with the generals in Algeria extended the reach of their power to Corsica and threatened even metropolitan France. The government of the Fourth Republic appealed to Charles de Gaulle as a figure of tremendous national prestige who could once again unite the divided nation. De Gaulle agreed to return to power and again not only brought the country together, but also did so through a period of transition that resulted in both the promulgation of a new constitution & democratic elections, which legitimated de Gaulle's position as head of state. De Gaulle's prestige however was not enough to heal the wounds caused by the crisis or to create, if not restore, full confidence in the government. This not least because, as Maurice Blanchot succinctly put it in his book, *L'Amitié* (Friendship, 1971), de Gaulle's return to power was "brought about not by the Resistance this time but by the mercenaries."[41] The colonial wars in Indochina *&* Algeria — not least because they were both all but inevitable failures — were perceived as being at once indignities and atrocities, parallel shames.

This perception intensified with the publication of Henri Alleg's memoir, *La Question* (The Question), by Éditions de Minuit in 1958. The book recounted, in chilling detail, the author's experience of being tortured by French military police in Algiers for one month during the summer of 1957. Alleg, a communist, had been a journalist and was the editor of a newspaper sympathetic to the Algerian nationalist cause. Éditions de Minuit had been founded during World War Two explicitly for the purpose of publishing writings associated with the resistance like Vercors' *The Silence of the Sea*. With the publication of *The Question*, the legacy of the resistance, of the struggle against oppression on behalf of individual freedom and human dignity, split in two, becoming a national narrative de Gaulle *&* others continued to codify and exploit as well as a political stance that would increasingly be used against him and against the French government. After *The Question*, the very notion of resistance was for many years more often seen as a struggle *against* the government of France than on behalf of it.

The irony of this shifting legacy directly impacted *Army of Shadows* a decade later when the French filmmaker Jean-Pierre Melville realized his long-standing dream of bringing a version of the book to the screen. Melville (1917–1973) was, like Kessel, of both French and Jewish heritage. Born Jean-Pierre Grumbach, he adopted the name Melville as *nom de guerre* while active in the resistance in World War Two and kept it as a stage-name after the war. Melville first encountered Kessel's novel in London in 1943, though filming it would take another twenty-five years. "*Army of Shadows* is the book on the Resistance," he said, "it's the most beautiful and the most complete of the documents on that tragic period in the history of humanity."[42] Perhaps daunted by the challenges proposed by either the collage structure or the moral ambiguity of *Army of Shadows*, Melville's first film was nevertheless another film version of a classic novel of resistance, Vercors' *The Silence of the Sea*, released in 1949. Over the next twenty years, films like *Bob le Flambeur* (1956), *Léon Morin, Priest* (1961), and *Le Samouraï* (1967) made Melville's name as a director of almost astonishingly stylized & stylish thrillers, several starring Alain Delon. *Army of Shadows* fit perfectly into Melville's *noir* world. His film condenses some of the characters and much of the plot into a more straightforward and linear thriller, filmed with his usual capacity to evoke the ambiguity, complicity, and community of the underground, as well as a sense of paranoid claustrophobia and tense suspense. Melville's background and personal and professional orientation made him an ideal director for the film

& those things played no small part in convincing Kessel to give the project his blessing.

Released in 1969, Melville's *Army of Shadows* sought to capitalize on the recent success of other films about the French resistance, most notably *Is Paris Burning?* (René Clément, dir., 1966), which had been a huge hit. Unfortunately the political landscape in France had again shifted. In May 1968, protests by students rapidly spread to factories and among other workers, culminating in a series of general strikes that once again threatened France with the possibility of civil war. Charles de Gaulle even fled the country briefly at the end of the month, his prestige and popularity clearly exhausted as marching students & workers chanted "Adieu de Gaulle!" (Goodbye de Gaulle). These events dissipated as workers' unions reached compromises with the government and factory owners. De Gaulle however would not recover. He resigned as President of the Republic in April 1969, only a few months before Melville's *Army of Shadows* reached the screen. Needless to say, the viewing public & perhaps more importantly the film critics were in no mood to celebrate a film that celebrated de Gaulle or Gaullism. Quite the contrary in fact, that same year, Marcel Ophuls released his shattering documentary, *Le Chagrin et la pitié* (*The Sorrow and the Pity*), offering an extremely nuanced & complex, though ultimately damning portrait of both collaboration and resistance during the occupation. The film was both nominated for an Academy Award and banned from distribution on French television for ten years. But its success and scandal signaled that, a generation after the events themselves, the French public was beginning to be ready to ask more complex questions of its history.

The failure of *Army of Shadows* among the critics impacted its foreign distribution. It would not be released to cinemas in the United States for more than forty-five years. When it was released, and not just released, restored, in 2006, the film was finally recognized as a masterpiece within Melville's oeuvre, appearing on many critics' top ten lists for the year. In the intervening years, cinema had been established as an art, as perhaps *the* art form of the twentieth century, and the war had passed to the farthest limits of living memory, its atrocities and its heroes considered *&* reconsidered in cyclical turn, as life yielded to memory *&* memory to the politics of memory.

The myth of the resistance, created and codified in books like *Army of Shadows*, continued after the war in the memoirs of resistors, many of whom were personally and politically motivated to tell their stories, in some cases, to settle old scores. Testimony of less prominent figures was gathered in oral and written archives in the decades after the war and again, in another wave of interviews, after the collapse of Gaullism following 1968. The focus of interest by historians and the public shifted over the years as well, emphasizing in turn different aspects of the resistance and of the World War Two era, from the initial myth, to the problem of collaboration, to the role of France in the Shoah, to the significant role of women in the resistance. When Jean-Luc Godard released his own cinematic meditation on the war, the resistance, *&*

the politics of memory, *Éloge de l'amour* (In Praise of Love, 2001), he layered the work in complex questions without simple answers or satisfactions. "When fact becomes legend, we must obey the legend," his characters lament. [43]

Encountering *Army of Shadows* now, perhaps once again especially now, raises a number of daunting, and indeed haunting, questions: the question of resistance — what is worth fighting for? —; the question of France, linked inexorably to that of fundamental human rights; the question of cosmopolitanism, of belongingness, of the relationship between self & neighbor, of guest & host, refugee & refuge; the question of human potential and of the malleability of humankind.

At one point in *Army of Shadows*, Augustine Viellat, the farmer's wife who agrees to hide the pilots and other refugees as they await their embarkation for Gibraltar, reflects that the whole episode, even as she is living it, strikes her as a kind of story or fable that she will one day recount to her grandchildren. Primo Levi made a similar observation in his memoir of Auschwitz, *If This Is a Man* (1947), about the personal stories the prisoners at Auschwitz recounted to one another:

> He told me his story, and today I have forgotten it, but it was certainly a sorrowful, cruel, and moving story; because such are all our stories, hundreds of thousands of stories, all different, and all full of a tragic, shocking necessity. We tell them to one another in the evening, & they take place in Norway,

Italy, Algeria, Ukraine – simple and incomprehensible, like the stories in the Bible. But are not they, too, stories in a new Bible? If these stories & fables sketch the outline of a new Bible, it is surely both secular and tragic, without the promise of a transcendent hero or final deliverance.[44]

Army of Shadows ends in the middle of the war. The first edition appeared in print prior to the liberation of Paris. At that moment, in that context, the text served a testimonial purpose but also a motivational one, as fuel for a burning fire. With this new edition, it still can.

NOTES

All translations are my own unless otherwise indicated.

01. Plato, *Republic*, bk. 3, 386b-c.

02. Joseph Kessel, *Ami, entends-tu* (Gallimard, La Table Ronde, Folio, 2006) 233.

03. Kessel, *Ami, entends-tu*, 240.

04. Joseph Kessel, Interview, *Combat* (5 juin 1969); reprinted in Kessel, *Reportages, Romans* (Gallimard, Quarto, 2010) 1262.

05. Joseph Kessel, "Le Sac de Balgriggan" (1920) reprinted in *Reportages, Romans*, 379.

06. Yves Courrière, *Joseph Kessel, ou sur la piste du lion* (Plon, 1985) 511.

07. *The Crew*, tr. André Naffis-Sahely (London: Pushkin Press, 2016).

08. Kessel, *Reportages, Romans*, 1262.

09. Courrière, *Joseph Kessel*, 450.

10. *Entretiens de Joseph Kessel avec Dominique Fabre, en 1952. Un Témoin inspiré* (Éditions Zoé-RSR [Radio Suisse romande], 2008). Quoted in Kessel, *Reportages, Romans*, 83.

11. Quoted in Yves Courrière, *Joseph Kessel*, 540.

12. Joseph Kessel, *L'Heure des châtiments: Reportages 1938–1945* (Tallandier, 2010) 147.

13. Robert Gildea, *Fighters in the Shadows: A New History of the French Resistance* (Harvard, 2015) 239.

14. Albert Camus, *The Rebel: An Essay on Man in Revolt* (1951) trans. Anthony Bower (Knopf, 1956) 4.

15. Gildea, *Fighters in the Shadows*, 115.

16. Jean Améry, *At the Mind's Limits* (1966) tr. Sidney Rosenfeld & Stella P. Rosenfeld (Indiana University Press, 1980) 12–13.

17. Gildea, *Fighters in the Shadows*, 130 ff.

18. On this network, see Thomas Rabino, *Le Réseau Carte: histoire d'un réseau de la Résistance, antiallemand, antigaulliste, anticommuniste et anticollaborationniste* (Perrin, 2008).

19. For additional information on Kessel's resistance activities, see Yves Courrière, *Joseph Kessel, 550–62*.

20. Kessel, *Ami-entends tu*, 303.

21. For more on this letter, see Emmanuelle Loyer, *Paris à New York: Intellectuels et artistes français en exil, 1940–1947* (Grasset, 2005) 103–4.

22. Antoine Saint-Exupéry, "An Open Letter to Frenchmen Everywhere," *New York Times Magazine* (November 29, 1943) 35; quoted in Anne Simonin, "La Résistance sans fiction? *L'Armée des ombres* (1943)" in Bruno Curatolo and François Marcot, ed. *Écrire sous l'Occupation: Du non-consentement à la Résistance France-Belgique-Pologne, 1940–1945* (Presses Universitaires de Rennes, 2011) 243.

23. Kessel, *Ami, entends-tu*, 337.

24. Kessel, *Ami, entends-tu*, 337–8.

25. For a selection of these articles, see Kessel, *L'Heure des châtiments*, 145–93.

26. Anne Simonin, "La Résistance sans fiction? *L'Armée des ombres* (1943)," *Écrire sous-L'Occupation*, 242.

27. Joseph Kessel, "Le visage de la grande espérance", *La Marseillaise* (Alger) № 39 (7 mars 1943). This article is not reprinted in either *L'Heure des Châtiments* or in *Army of Shadows*.

28. Kessel, *L'Heure des Châtiments*, 175.

29. Productive comparison can be made between *Army of Shadows* and later English language works of a similar type, including Norman Mailer's *Armies of the Night* (1968) and *The Executioner's Song* (1979), and Truman Capote's *In Cold Blood* (1966).

30. See Courrière, *Joseph Kessel,* 590; Gildea, *Fighters in the Shadows,* 322; and Simonin, "La Résistance sans fiction? *L'Armée des Ombres,*" 244–6. Simonin offers an effective comparison between Kessel's version of events from the life of Jacques Médéric and Lucie Aubrac's recounting of similar events in her article, "Jacques Médéric," *La France Libre* № 44 (15 juin 1944) 100–1. Aubrac did not arrive in London until after Kessel published *Army of Shadows,* suggesting, according to Simonin, that Kessel learned of these events from Médéric himself.

31. Hannah Arendt, "Civil Disobedience," *Crises of the Republic* (Harcourt Brace & Company, 1972) 88.

32. Arendt, "Civil Disobedience," 80.

33. Jean-Paul Sartre, "The Republic of Silence" (1944) in Sartre, *The Aftermath of War* (1948) tr. Chris Turner (Seagull, 2008) 4.

34. Albert Camus, *Letters to a German Friend* (1945) in *Resistance, Rebellion, and Death* (1960) tr. Justin O'Brien (Alfred Knopf, 1960) 6–7.

35. André Malraux, *La Politique, la Culture. Discours, articles, entretiens* (Gallimard, 1996) 297. Quoted in Gildea, *Fighters in the Shadows,* 452.

36. Sartre, "The Republic of Silence," 6.

37. For full details of these publications, see Simonin, "La Résistance sans fiction? *L'Armée des Ombres,*" 252–3. The only chapter not published separately was the final one.

38. On Jacques Schiffrin, Pantheon, and the resistance, see André Schiffrin, *The Business of Books* (Verso, 2000) 17–19.

39. Haakon Chevalier was a professor of Romance languages at the University of California at Berkeley from 1927 to 1949. In addition to *Army of Shadows,* he translated books by and about André Malraux, Louis Aragon, Salvador Dali, Jean Dubuffet, Franz Fanon, and others. Chevalier was also a close friend of J. Robert Oppenheimer who taught at Berkeley for many years. According to Chevalier, the two were members of a group

affiliated with the communist party there from 1938 to 1942. In 1942, Chevalier was approached by a Soviet agent who hoped to use him as a means to gain access to Oppenheimer who was then the head of the Los Alamos Labs, the research site of the Manhattan Project, which developed the first atomic bomb. In 1947, these connections led to Chevalier being called before the House Subcommittee on Un-American Activities after which point he lost his position at Berkeley and left the United States. He spent the rest of his life writing and translating books in France. These connections also contributed to the revocation of Oppenheimer's own security clearance in 1954. For details about Chevalier and Oppenheimer, see in particular, Greg Herken, *The Brotherhood of the Bomb* (Henry Holt, 2002). These facts are relevant here as testimony to the politics surrounding even the original translation of *Army of Shadows*.

40. A third variant "preface" to the book appeared separately in *L'Arche* (février 1944) 69–72.

41. Blanchot, *Friendship* (1971) tr. Elizabeth Rottenberg (Stanford University Press, 1997) 297.

42. Jean-Pierre Melville, *Le Cinéma selon Jean-Pierre Melville: Entretiens avec Rui Nogueira* (Petit Bibliothèque des Cahiers du cinema, 1996) 163–164.

43. See Jean-Luc Godard, *In Praise of Love* in Godard, *Phrases: Six Films* (Contra Mundum Press, 2016) 291. The line is a paraphrase of a line from *The Man Who Shot Liberty Valance* (John Ford, dir., 1962).

44. Primo Levi, *If This Is a Man* (1947) tr. Stuart Woolf in *The Complete Works of Primo Levi*, vol. 1 (Liveright Publishing Company, 2015) 62.

PREFACE

There is no propaganda and there is no fiction in this book. No detail has been forced, and none have been invented. You will find collected here, without formality and sometimes even randomly, only authentic, proven, verified, and thus commonplace facts. The current events of French life.

The sources are numerous and trustworthy. For the characters, the situations, the most naked suffering and the simplest courage, there was then a tragic embarrassment of choices. In these conditions the task seemed much easier.

Yet, of all the works that I have written in the course of an already long life, there is not one that has demanded of me as many sorrows as this one. And none left me as discontented.

I wanted to say so much and I said so little.

Safety was naturally the first obstacle. Those who want to write about the resistance without romanticism & without ever resorting to the imagination are chained by their civic duties. It is not that novels or poetry appear less true than stories bound to reality. I rather believe the contrary. But we live in complete horror, in the midst of bloodshed. I don't feel that I have the right or the strength to supersede the simplicity of the chronicle, the humility of the document.

It was then necessary that in approach everything had to be precise & highly scrupulous. A single false color risked giving a Saint-Sulpician tone to the paintings of the sacred struggle.

Everything needed to be precise &, at the same time, nothing must be recognizable.

Because of the enemy, its informers, its minions, it was necessary to disguise faces, to uproot people and plant them elsewhere, mixing episodes, constraining voices, separating links, concealing the secrets of attack and defense.

One could speak freely then only of the dead (when they had neither family nor friends who were endangered) or of stories that are so familiar in France that they reveal nothing to anyone.

Are the tracks well entangled, effaced? Will no one recognize this or that person? Such is the fear that continually suspended or hindered my hand. And when it had been appeased, when I thought I had taken every required precaution, another anxiety was born. I asked myself then: "Am I still being truthful? Had I found just equivalents when transposing origins, habits, professions, familial relations and feelings?" For an act no longer has the same character, the same value, or the same meaning, if it is accomplished by a rich or a poor person, a bachelor or a father of six, an old man or a young girl.

And when I believed I had almost succeeded in this substitution, I was seized by a bitter sadness. There was nothing left of this man, of this woman whom I loved, whom I admired, whose life or death I wanted to recount in their name, with their true face. So I tried to at least reproduce the sound of laughter, the quality of a gaze, or the whisper of a voice.

———————

Such was the first difficulty. Obviously. And so that's to say of a material kind. But the obvious and material inconveniences are never the heaviest to bear. Another torment had pursued me while I was writing these pages. It had nothing to do with safety requirements. It was of a personal nature.

Without any false modesty, I had constantly felt my inferiority, my misery as a writer before the profound heart of this book, before the image and the spirit of the great, wonderful mystery that is the French Resistance.

Is there a writer who, in trying to paint a landscape, a light, a character or a destiny, has not suffered an assault of despair? Who does not feel unfaithful to the colors of nature, to the essence of light? Above or below the human being? Close to the thread of fate?

What, then, when it comes to recounting the story of France, an obscure, secret France, which is new to its friends, its enemies, & new especially to itself?

France no longer has bread, wine, fire. But mainly it no longer has any laws. Civil disobedience, individual or organized rebellion, have become duties to the fatherland. The national hero is the clandestine man, the outlaw.

Nothing about the order imposed by the enemy and by the Marshal is valid. Nothing counts. Nothing is true any more. One changes home, name, every day. Officials and police officers are helping insurgents. One finds accomplices even in ministries. Prisons, getaways, tortures, bombings, scuffles. One dies & kills as if it's natural.

France lives, bleeds, in all its depths. It is toward the shadow that its true and unknown face is turned. In the catacombs of revolt, people create their own light and find their own law.

Never has France waged a nobler and more beautiful war than in the basements where it prints its free newspapers, in its nocturnal lands, and in its secret coves where it received its free friends and from where its free children set out, in torture cells where, despite tongs, red-hot pins, & crushed bones, the French died as free men.

Everything that one will read herein has been lived by the people of France.

My sole wish is to not have rendered their image with too much infidelity.

1

THE ESCAPE

It was raining. The armored car advanced & slowly descended the slippery road that followed the curves of the hills. Gerbier was alone in the interior of the car with a gendarme. Another gendarme was driving. The one who was guarding Gerbier had the cheeks of a farmer and a rather strong odor.

As the car turned into a side road, the gendarme observed:

— We make a little detour, but I don't think you're in a hurry.

— Truly not, said Gerbier, with a half-smile.

The armored car stopped before an isolated farm.

Gerbier saw, through the barred window, a bit of the sky and a field. He heard the driver get out.

— It won't be long, said the gendarme. My partner is going to get some provisions. You have to manage as you can in these times of misery.

— It's only natural, said Gerbier.

The gendarme gazed at his prisoner and nodded his head. He was a well-dressed man and he had a frank manner, a comely face. What times of misery... He wasn't the first whom the gendarme was embarrassed to see in handcuffs.

— You won't be too badly off in the camp! said the gendarme. I'm not talking about the food, of course. Before the war the dogs would've gone for want. But aside from that, it's the best concentration camp in France, so they say. It's the German camp.

— I don't catch your drift, said Gerbier.

— During the phony war, we expected, I think, to have many prisoners, the gendarme explained. We had set up a big center for them in the country. Naturally not a single one came. But today, it's put to good use.

— In short, a lucky shot, Gerbier remarked.

— As you say, Monsieur, as you say! exclaimed the gendarme.

The driver returned to his seat. The armored car went off again. The rain continued to fall on the Limousin countryside.

———

Gerbier, his hands free, but standing at attention, was waiting for the camp commandant to address him. The commandant was reading Gerbier's dossier. Sometimes, he would dig the thumb of his left hand into the hollow of his cheek and slowly withdraw it. The fat, soft, and unhealthy flesh kept the white imprint a few seconds & again swelled painfully like an old sponge devoid of elasticity. This movement marked the tempo of the commandant's reflections.

"Always the same thing," he thought. "We don't know who we receive, nor how to treat them."

He sighed at the memory of the pre-war, and the time when he was a prison warden. He only had to be prudent about profits made on food. Nothing else presented any difficulty. The prisoners ranked themselves into known categories and each corresponded to a code of conduct. Now, on the contrary, one could get as big a cut of camp rations (nobody worried), but it was a headache to separate the populace. Some who arrived without judgments or sentences remained indefinitely imprisoned. Others, with terrible records, got out very quickly and regained influence in the department, the regional prefecture, or even at Vichy.

The commandant didn't look at Gerbier. He had given up making opinions based on faces and clothing. He was trying to read between the lines, in the police notes that the gendarmes gave him when they delivered their prisoner.

"Independent character, quick mind; remote and ironic," read the commandant. And he translated: "to subdue." Then: "Distinguished Bridge & Highway Engineer," and, his thumb in his cheek, the commandant said: "to spare."

"Suspected of Gaullist activities" — "to subdue, to subdue." — But then: "Released for lack of evidence" — "influence, influence … to spare."

The commandant sank his thumb deeper into his adipose flesh. It seemed to Gerbier that the cheek would never return to its normal condition. However, the edema gradually disappeared. Then the commandant declared with a certain solemnity:

— I'll put you in a building that was intended for German officers.

— I am very sensitive to this honor, said Gerbier.

For the first time the commandant directed his heavy &
vague gaze — that of a man who eats too much — toward
the face of his new prisoner.

The prisoner was smiling, but only half way — his lips
were thin and contracted.

"To spare, certainly," thought the camp commandant, "but
to spare with wariness."

The quartermaster gave Gerbier sabots & a red cloth blouson.

— This was intended, he began, for the prisoners ...

— The Germans, I know, said Gerbier.

He took off his clothes, put on the short blouson. Then,
at the doorstep of the shop, he scanned the camp with his
eyes. It was a flush, grassy field around which the undulations
of the uninhabited terrain came together & separated. Rain
was still falling from the low sky. Evening was approaching.
The rings of barbed wire and the patrol path that separated them were already harshly lit. But the unequally sized
buildings scattered across the field remained dark. Gerbier
walked toward one of the smallest of them.

The barrack harbored five red blousons.

The colonel, the pharmacist, and the traveling salesman,

sitting like Turks near the door, were playing dominœs with pieces of cardboard on the back of a mess tin. The two other prisoners were in the back talking in low voices.

Armel was stretched out on his straw mattress and wrapped in the sole blanket that was granted to the internees. Legrain had spread his over him, but it didn't keep Armel from shivering. He had still lost a lot of blood during the afternoon. His blond hair was matted with sweat from a fever. His fleshless face bore an expression of a rather confined but inalterable sweetness.

— I assure you, Roger, I assure you that if you could only have faith, you wouldn't be unhappy, because you'd no longer be so rebellious, murmured Armel.

— But I want to be, I want to, said Legrain.

He clenched his thin fists and a sort of hissing emerged from his collapsed chest. He resumed with furor:

— You came here, you were twenty, I was seventeen. We were healthy, we did harm to no one, we only wanted to live. Look at us today. And what's happening all around! That such exists and that there's a God, I cannot understand it.

Armel had shut his eyes. His features were as if worn away by an inner fatigue and a growing shadow.

— It's only with God that everything becomes comprehensible, he answered.

Armel and Legrain were among the camp's first internees. And Legrain had no other friend in the world. He wanted to do everything to ensure the recovery of this bloodless and angelic figure. It inspired him with tenderness and mercy, his sole bonds with men. But there was in him an even stronger feeling — and inflexible — which prevented him from consenting to Armel's murmuring.

— No. I cannot believe in God, he said. It's too convenient for those bastards to pay in the next world. I want to see justice on this earth. I want…

The movement at the doorway of the barrack stopped Legrain. A new blouson had just entered.

— My name is Philippe Gerbier, said the new arrival.

Colonel Jarret du Plessis, Aubert the pharmacist, and Octave Bonnafous, the traveling salesman, introduced themselves one after the other.

— I don't know, Monsieur, what brings you here, said the colonel.

— I don't know either, said Gerbier half smiling.

— But I want you to know right away why I was interned, continued the colonel. I had declared in a café that Admiral Darlan was a Jack Fool. Yes.

The colonel made a rather emphatic pause and continued strongly:

— Today, I add that Marshal Pétain is another Jack Fool who lets soldiers be bullied by sailors. Yes!

— At least you suffer for an idea, colonel! exclaimed the traveling salesman. But me, for my work, I simply passed by a square where there was a Gaullist demonstration …

— And me, interrupted Aubert the pharmacist, it's even worse for me.

He abruptly asked Gerbier:

— Do you know what a Malher shell is?

— No, said Gerbier.

— That general ignorance has killed me, replied Aubert. The Malher shell, Monsieur, is a container in the shape of an ogival mold, meant to produce chemical reactions under pressure. I'm an expert chemist, Monsieur. I couldn't help but have a Malher shell, after all. I'd been denounced for possessing shells. I could never make myself heard by the authorities.

— There are no authorities, there are only Jack Fools! Yes, said the colonel, they discontinued my pension.

Gerbier realized that he would hear these stories a hundred times. With extreme politesse he asked where the place was that he was to occupy in the barrack. The colonel, who was functioning as the barrack master, pointed to a free straw mattress in the back. When carrying his suitcase there, Gerbier approached his other companions. He held out his hand to Legrain. He gave his name and said:

— Communist.

— Already? asked Gerbier.

Legrain blushed deep red and replied very quickly:

— I was too young to have my party card, that's right, but it's the same thing. I was arrested with my father and other militants. The others were sent elsewhere. Here, it seems, life was too sweet for them. I asked to go with them, but they wouldn't let me.

— Long ago? Gerbier asked again.

— Immediately after the armistice.

— That makes for close to a year, said Gerbier.

— I'm the oldest in the camp, said Legrain.

— The most longstanding, Gerbier corrected, smiling.

— After me, it's Armel, Legrain said … The young teacher who's lying down.

— He's sleeping? asked Gerbier.

— No, he's very ill, Legrain murmured. A bad case of dysentery.

— And the infirmary? asked Gerbier.

— There's no room, said Legrain.

At their feet a gentle, exhausted voice spoke.

— To die, anywhere is good enough.

— Why are you here? Gerbier asked, leaning over Armel.

— I swore that I would never be able to teach children hatred of the Jews and the Brits, said the teacher, without strength enough to open his eyes.

Gerbier stood up. He showed no emotion. Only his lips turned a slightly darker color.

Gerbier put his suitcase at the head of the straw mattress assigned to him. The barrack was completely devoid of furniture and accessories, except, in the center, the inevitable latrine bucket for the night.

— That was all that was necessary for the German officers, who never came, said the colonel. But the warden and the guards helped themselves and the rest went from the barracks to the black market.

— Do you play dominœs? the pharmacist asked Gerbier.

— No, sorry, he said.

— We can teach you, the traveling salesman proposed.

— Thank you, a thousand times, but I really don't have the least disposition for it, said Gerbier.

— Then you'll excuse us, exclaimed the colonel. There's just enough time for a game, before night falls.

The darkness came. Roll was called. The doors were shut. There was no light in the barrack. Legrain's breathing was wheezy and oppressed. In his corner, the little delirious teacher hardly made a sound. Gerbier thought: "The camp commandant isn't so inept. He stifles me between three idiots & two lost children."

———

The next day, when Legrain left the barracks, it was raining. Despite this, and despite the freshness of the April morning air on a field exposed to the winds, Gerbier, naked in his sabots and with a towel around his waist, did his exercises. His body was of a matte color, its consistency dry and hard. His muscles weren't visible, but their united, compact mobility evoked the sensation of a difficult to carve block of stone. Legrain considered those movements with sadness. Merely deep breathing made his lungs whistle like a hollow bladder … Gerbier shouted between two exercises:

— Already out walking!

— I'm going to the camp power plant, said Legrain. I work there.

Gerbier finished flexing & approached Legrain.

— A good job? he asked him.

A deep red flush came over Legrain's sunken cheeks. It was, at times, the only trace of his great youth. For the rest, the deprivations, confinement, and especially the constant fatigue of a heavy and haunting inner revolt, had aged his face and his demeanor terribly.

— I don't even get a crust of bread for my work, said Legrain. But I love the job and I don't want to lose the touch. And that's all there is to it.

Gerbier's aquiline nose was very slender at the bridge. Because of this, his eyes seemed very close together. When Gerbier looked at someone attentively, as he did at this moment with Legrain, his eternal half-smile became fixed in a severe fold, and it was as if his eyes melted into a single black fire. As Gerbier remained silent, Legrain turned on his sabots. Gerbier said softly:

— Goodbye, comrade.

Legrain wheeled round and faced him with such abruptness that it was as if he had been burned.

— You're … you're … a communist, he stammered.

— No, I'm not a communist, said Gerbier.

He let a second pass and added with a smile:

— But that doesn't prevent me from having comrades.

Gerbier tightened his towel around his waist & resumed his exercises. Legrain's red blouson slowly faded out on the rainy field.

———

In the afternoon, when the sky cleared up a bit, Gerbier made a round of the camp. It took him several hours. The field was immense and entirely occupied by the city of internees. One could see that it had grown in a disorderedly manner, in fits & starts, and as Vichy's orders progressively drained the ever-growing population of captives toward this high stretch of bare ground. In the middle was the original nucleus that from the beginning had been built for German prisoners. Its buildings were decent and solid. The penitentiary administration offices were set up in the best of them. Then wooden, corrugated iron and tarred barracks ranged as far as the eye could see. It resembled the leprous zones that surround great cities. It had taken space, again more space, always more space.

For foreigners. For traffickers. For Freemasons. For Kabyles. For opponents of the Legion. For Jews. For peasant deserters. For gypsies. For former convicts. For political suspects. For those of suspicious intent. For those who embarrassed the government. For those they feared would influence the people. For those who had been denounced without proof. For those who had served their sentences and whom they would not set free. For those whom the judges refused to condemn, to judge, & who were punished for their innocence …

There were hundreds of men who were taken from their families, from their work, from their cities, from their truths, and herded into camps for an indeterminate period on the simple decision of officials, like wrecks on a muddy beach beyond the range of the sea.

To guard those men whose legions daily increased, they had need of yet other men, who grew ever more numerous. They had been recruited randomly, in haste, from among the dregs of the unemployed, the good-for-nothings, alcoholics, degenerates. For uniforms, they had their wretched clothes, a beret, and an armband. They were very poorly paid. Those outcasts suddenly had power. They showed themselves to be fierce. They made money out of everything: starvation rations were halved, tobacco, soap, toiletries, basic items — they sold everything at outrageous prices. Corruption was the sole thing that had any effect on these guards.

During his walk Gerbier was able to win over two procurers. He also exchanged some words with internees lying in front of their barracks. He had the feeling of approaching a kind of mold, of reddish mushrooms in human form. Those undernourished people, floating & shivering in their blousons, unemployed, unshaven, unwashed, had vacant and empty eyes and limp mouths with no elasticity. Gerbier thought that this complete neglect was natural. Real insurgents, when they were taken, were usually held in deep and silent prisons, or handed over to the Gestapo. Even in this camp there were no doubt a few resolute men who did not yield to deterioration. But it would take time to identify them, in the midst of this immense flock, broken by adversity. Gerbier remembered Legrain, his exhausted but unyielding face, his courageous, emaciated shoulders. Yet it was he who had spent the greatest number of months in the retting trough.

Gerbier walked toward the power station that was located among the central buildings, known in the camp as the German quarter.

As he closed in on it, Gerbier crossed a file of skeletal Kabyles pushing wheelbarrows loaded with garbage cans. They moved very slowly. Their wrists seemed on the verge of breaking. Their heads were too heavy for their emaciated, birdlike necks. One of them stumbled and his wheelbarrow toppled, overturning the garbage can. Peelings, sordid remains, scattered on the ground. Before Gerbier knew what was happening, he saw a kind of mute, rabid horde panic, throw itself on the waste. Then he saw another horde come running. The guards started beating them with their fists, their feet, cudgels, coshes. First they struck to establish order and out of duty. But they quickly took pleasure in it and throttled away as if intoxicated. They aimed at fragile & vulnerable areas — stomachs, kidneys, livers, sex organs. They abandoned their victims only when they had become inanimate.

Gerbier suddenly heard Legrain's muffled & wheezing voice.

— It makes me crazy to think that we went searching for those wretches and took them from their homes in Africa. They were told of France, beautiful France, and of the Marshal, the good grandfather. They were promised ten francs a day; at the construction sites they only got half of that. They asked why. Then they were sent here. They croak like flies. And when they haven't had time to croak, this is what happens …

Breathless, Legrain coughed a long hollow cough.

— All debts will be paid, said Gerbier.

His half-smile was at this moment one of extreme acuity. Most people felt discomfort when this expression passed over Gerbier's features. But it inspired great confidence in Legrain.

———————

Toward the middle of May, beautiful weather began to take hold for good. Late spring burst forth all at once in full strength. Thousands of small flowers shot up in the grass of the field. The internees began to take sunbaths. Sharp hip-bones, protruding ribs, flaccid skin, arms reduced to the form of bones rested among all the fresh flowers. Gerbier, who roamed the field all day long, constantly collided with this hospital humanity stunned by spring. No one could tell if he felt disgust, pity, or indifference for it. He himself didn't know. But when, at midday, he saw Legrain exposing himself like others to the heat, Gerbier quickly went to him.

— Don't do that, and cover yourself right away, he said.

Since Legrain didn't obey, Gerbier threw a blouson over the young man's pitiful torso.

— I hear you whistling and coughing in your sleep, said Gerbier. You surely have something in your lungs. The sun is very dangerous for you.

Gerbier had never seemed interested in Legrain more than in the pharmacist or the colonel of their barrack.

— You don't look like a doctor, said Legrain with aston-ishment.

— And I'm not, said Gerbier, but I oversaw the installation of a power line in Savoy. There were tuberculosis institutions there. I used to talk with the doctors.

Legrain's eyes lit up. He exclaimed:

— You're in electricity?

— Like you, said Gerbier cheerfully.

— Oh no! I see that you're a master of the trade, said Legrain. But we could talk shop all the same.

Legrain was afraid to appear indiscreet and added:

— From time to time.

— Immediately, if you want, said Gerbier.

— He lay down near Legrain and while chewing blades of grass and flower stems, listened to the young man talk about the electrical station where he worked.

— Would you like me to take you there? Legrain finally asked.

Gerbier saw a rudimentary but solid station run with knowledge and distinction. Gerbier also saw Legrain's assistant. He was an old Austrian engineer, of Jewish origin. He had fled from Vienna to Prague and from Prague to France. He was very timid. He tried to make himself as small as possible. After so many adversities & fears, he seemed satisfied with his fate.

The estimation that Gerbier had made of this man allowed him to appreciate the entire magnitude of a scene that unfolded some time later.

A Gestapo car stopped before the entrance to the concentration camp. The gates were lifted. Some guards in berets and with armbands mounted the running boards and the grey car rolled slowly toward the German quarter. When it had come close to the power plant, an S.S. officer stepped out and motioned to the guards to follow him inside the building. It was sunbathing time. Many prisoners approached the car. The uniformed driver was smoking a cigar and blowing smoke through the nostrils of his wide, flat nose. He did not look at the bay of emaciated, half-naked, and silent men. Amid the silence, there was a scream, and another, and again another. Then they merged into a single lamentation, which was very close to the plaint of an animal. The half-naked men started to panic. But the fascination for horror was stronger in them than fear. They waited. The guards dragged a white haired man out of the building. The old engineer was struggling, still shouting. Suddenly he saw the bay of half-naked, silent, and pale men. He began to utter broken words. Only a few phrases were distinguishable: "French soil ... French government ... free zone ... asylum ..."

Gerbier, who at first kept at a distance from the spectators, didn't notice that he was approaching them, crossing the last row, crossing the next, that he was reaching the first, that he was still advancing. A trembling and warm hand landed on his wrist. Gerbier's body suddenly relaxed and his eyes lost their fixed expression.

— Thank you, he said to Legrain.

Gerbier breathed very hard. After that he looked, with a kind of avid hatred, at how the guards threw the old engineer into the car, and how the driver continued to blow smoke rings through his wide nostrils.

— Thank you, Gerbier said again.

He smiled at Legrain with that half-smile, where the eyes had no part.

That evening, in the barrack, Legrain wanted to speak of the incident but Gerbier avoided all conversation. It was the same the following days. Besides, Armel the teacher grew sicker and sicker and Legrain had no other thought but for his friend.

———

The young teacher died one night with no more than his usual delirium. Early in the morning some Kabyles took his body away. Legrain went to work. The day passed and he behaved no differently than the day before. When he returned to the barrack, the colonel, the pharmacist, and the traveling salesman stopped playing dominœs and wanted to console him.

— I'm not sad, said Legrain. Armel is better off that way.

Gerbier said nothing to Legrain. He gave him the pack of cigarettes that he had bought from a guard in the afternoon. Legrain smoked three in quick succession, despite his exhausting cough. Night came. Roll call was made. The doors shut. The colonel, the traveling salesman, and the pharmacist went to sleep one after another. Legrain seemed peaceful. Gerbier fell asleep in turn.

He was awakened by a familiar noise. Legrain coughing. Gerbier could not yet manage to go back to sleep. He listened more attentively. And he understood — Legrain was forcing himself to cough to stifle the sputtering of his sobs. Gerbier searched for Legrain's hand & said to him in a very low voice:

— I'm here, old man.

Not a sound is made, nothing more is heard for several seconds from the place where Legrain's straw mattress was. "He's fighting for his dignity," thought Gerbier. He had guessed rightly. But Legrain was a child all the same. Gerbier suddenly felt a weightless body and small bony shoulders contract against him. He heard a barely audible groan.

— I have no one in the world... Armel has left me. He is perhaps with his good God now. He believed so strongly. But me, I cannot see him there ... I don't believe it, Monsieur Gerbier ... I beg your pardon ... but I can't continue. I've no one in the world. Talk to me from time to time, Monsieur Gerbier, will you?

Gerbier then whispered into Legrain's ear:

— We never let down a comrade of ours in the resistance.

Legrain had become silent.

— The resistance. You hear? Gerbier said again. You sleep with that word in your head. It's the most beautiful, in this time, in the whole French language. You can't know of it. It was made while they were destroying you here. Sleep, I promise to tell you about it.

———————

Gerbier accompanied Legrain to his job. They walked slowly and Gerbier was speaking:

— You understand, they've come in their tanks, with their empty eyes. They thought that their tank treads were made to trace the new law of peoples. Since they had manufactured many tanks, they had the assurance of having been born to write this law. They have a horror of freedom, of thinking. Their true war aim is the death of the thinking man, of the free man. They want to exterminate everyone who doesn't have empty eyes. In France they had found people who had the same interests and those people have gone into their service. And they put you here to rot, you who had not yet even begun to live. They caused the death of young Armel. You saw them hand over the poor guy who believed in the right of asylum. At the same time they announced that the conqueror was magnanimous. A foul old man tried to suborn the country. "Be wise, be acquiescent," he taught. "Forget that you have been proud, joyous, and free. Obey and smile at the victor. It will allow you to get by peacefully." The people who surrounded the old man were calculating that France was gullible and that it was soft. It is the country of measure and of balance. "France is so civilized, so weakened, they thought, it has lost the meaning of underground warfare and of secret death. If she accepts it, she will fall asleep. And in her sleep, we will put her eyes out." And they thought again: "We do not fear extremists. They have no connections. They have no weapons. And we have all the German divisions to defend us." While they were rejoicing then, the resistance was born.

ain walked on without daring to turn his head toward Gerbier. It was as if he were fearful of intervening in
the accomplishment of a miracle. This man so distant, so
miserly about everything, suddenly burst into fiery words ...
And the universe suddenly became a whole different universe ... Legrain saw the grass and the camp barracks and the
red blousons and the emaciated silhouettes of the Kabyles
dragging themselves about at their forced labor. But all this
was changing its form and function. The life of the camp no
longer ceased at the barbed wire fences. It extended to the
entire country. It became illuminated; it took on meaning.
The Kabyles and Armel and himself, they entered into a great
human order. Legrain felt himself gradually freed from this
blind, fierce, enchained, confused, obtuse, hopeless revolt
which struggled in him, tearing and ravaging all his substance.
He felt himself approaching a great mystery. And he was too
ignorant and too sickly to contemplate the companion who
was lifting the veils of this mystery for him.

— How it was done, I don't know, said Gerbier. I think
that no one will ever know. But a farmer had cut a telephone
wire in the country. An old woman had struck the legs of a
German soldier with her cane. Tracts circulated. A butcher
from La Villette had thrown a captain who was requisition-
ing meat with too much arrogance into a cold storage room. A
bourgeoisie gives a false address to the victors who are trying
to find their way. Railroad workers, priests, poachers, bank-
ers help escaped prisoners to get through by the hundreds.
Farmers harbor British soldiers. A prostitute refuses to sleep

with the conquerors. Officers, French soldiers, masons, paint-ers hide weapons. You knew nothing of all this. You were here. But for those who felt this awakening, the first stirring, it was the most moving thing in the world. It was the lifeblood of liberty that was beginning to spring up across French soil. Then the Germans and their servants and the old man, they decided to extirpate the wild plant. But the more they tore at it, the stronger it grew. They've filled the prisons. They've multiplied the camps. They've become frantic. They've im-prisoned the colonel, the traveling salesman, the pharmacist. And they've made even more enemies. They've gunned down. Yet, it was blood that the plant had most needed to grow and to spread. Blood has flowed. Blood is flowing. It will flow like a barrage. And the plant will become a forest.

Gerbier & Legrain went round the power plant. Gerbier said again:

— Those who enter the resistance aim at the Germans. At the same time they hit Vichy and its old man, and the old man's henchmen and the director of our camp, and the guards that you see every day at work. The resistance, it is all the French men who do not want the eyes of France to turn into dead eyes, into empty eyes.

———

Legrain and Gerbier were sitting in the grass. The wind from the hillsides was turning cool. Evening was coming; Gerbier spoke to the young man about the resistance newspapers.

— And the people who do dare to write what they think? asked Legrain, his cheeks inflamed.

— They can dare everything: they've no other law, no other master than their thought, said Gerbier. This thought is stronger in them than life. The men who publish those papers are unknown, but one day we will raise monuments to their work. They who find the paper risk death. They who write the articles risk death. And they who carry the newspapers risk death. Nothing can stop them. Nothing can stifle the cry that comes out of the Ronéo, hidden in pitiable bedrooms, put together by the presses, lurking in the depths of cellars. Don't think that those newspapers look like the ones that are sold openly. They are little, miserable squares of paper. Hardly welcome paper, typed or printed devil-may-care. The characters are dull. The headings meager. The ink often smudges. They make them as they can. One week in one town and one week in another. They take what lies at hand. But the newspaper appears. The articles follow underground routes. Someone collects them; someone secretly disposes them. Stealth crews do the layout. Police, snitches, spies, denouncers stir up: searching, snooping, sniffing. The newspaper is shared on the roads of France. It isn't great; it doesn't look impressive. It swells shabby, cracked, disjointed suitcases. But each of its lines is like a ray of gold. A ray of free thought.

— My father was a typographer ... so I understand, said Legrain. There can't be many of these newspapers.

— There's a mass of them, said Gerbier. Every major resistance movement has its own, and they turn out tens of thousands of them. And then there are those of the isolated groups. And those of the provinces. And doctors have theirs, and musicians, and students, and teachers, and professors, and painters, and writers, and engineers.

— And the communists? asked Legrain in a low voice.

— But naturally, they have "*L'Humanité*." As before.

— "*L'Huma*," said Legrain, "*L'Huma*"...

His hollow eyes were full of ecstasy. He tried to say more but a series of coughing fits prevented him.

———————

It was noon. The prisoners had swallowed the mess tin of dirty water that served as grub and lay motionless in the sun. Legrain stood with Gerbier in the shadow of the barrack.

— They know how to die in the resistance, Gerbier was saying. The daughter of an industrialist was to be executed by the Gestapo because she would reveal nothing about the organization to which she belonged. Her father obtained the favor of seeing her. He begged her to talk. She insulted him and *ordered* the German officer who was present at the interview to take her father away... A militant of the Christian syndicates made friends with the Germans, either out of weakness, or out of interest. His wife kicked him out. And his very young son enlisted in a militia. He engaged in sabotage, he killed some guards. When he was caught, he wrote to his mother: "Everything is clean. I die a good Frenchman *&* a good Christian." I saw the letter... A famous professor was arrested — thrown into a Gestapo cell in Fresnes. They tortured him to extract names. He resisted ... he resisted ... But finally, he was exhausted. He became afraid of himself. He tore up his shirt & hanged himself ... After a violent demonstration, where German blood flowed in Paris, a dozen men were sentenced to death. They were to be shot the following day at dawn. They knew it. And one of them, a worker, began to recount funny stories. All night *he made his comrades laugh*. It was the German prison chaplain who recounted those details to the worker's family.

Legrain looked away & asked hesitantly:

— Tell me ... Monsieur Gerbier ... weren't there any communists among those demonstrators?

— All of them were, answered Gerbier. There was also a communist, Gabriel Péri, who before dying left the perhaps most beautiful word of the resistance: "I am glad," he wrote. "We prepare tomorrows that sing."

Gerbier put his hand on Legrain's narrow wrist and said to him gently:

— I want you to understand me once and for all. There's no hatred, no suspicion, no barrier of any sort between the communists and other Frenchmen of today. We're all in the same fight, and it's the communists against whom the enemy is unremitting in the first place. We know it. And we know that they are as brave as the bravest and the best organized. They help us and we help them. They love us & we love them. Everything has become very simple.

— Speak, Monsieur Gerbier, speak again, murmured Legrain.

———————

It was mostly at night that Gerbier had time to talk.

Their tightly closed little barrack retained the heat that amassed throughout the length of the day. The straw mattresses burned the kidneys. And the darkness was suffocating. The companions in captivity turned and turned again in their sleep. But nothing mattered to Legrain, not even the whistling that rushed from his lungs that sometimes, without his noticing, forced him to compress his chest with both hands. And Gerbier spoke about how radio stations hidden in towns or in hamlets allowed them to talk every day with friends in the free world. He recounted the work of the secret operatives, their cunning, their patience, their risks, and the wonderful music that are the encrypted messages. He showed the immense network of listening posts and observers that enveloped the enemy, counted its regiments, broke its defenses, accessed its documents. And Gerbier also said that in every season, at every hour, liaison agents ran, walked, furtively wandered the whole of France. And he depicted this underground France, this France of hidden arms depots, of command posts ranging from refuge to refuge, of unknown leaders, of men and women who were constantly changing name, appearance, roof & face.

— Those people, Gerbier would say, could've kept quiet. Nothing forced them into action. Wisdom, common sense, would advise them to eat and sleep in the shadow of German bayonets and to watch their business flourish, their women smile, their children grow up. Material goods and the boons of close affection were thereby assured them. To appease &

lull their consciences, they even had the blessing of the old man of Vichy. Really, nothing forced them to fight, nothing but their free souls.

— Do you know, said Gerbier, what the life of the outlaw, of the man of the resistance, is like? He has no identity, or he has had so many that he forgot his own. He has no ration card. He can no longer even partially fuel his hunger. He sleeps in an attic, or in a streetwalker's house, or on the floor of a shop, or in an abandoned barn, or on a train-station bench. He can no longer see his own family because the police monitor them. If his wife — which often happens — is also in the resistance, his children grow up indiscriminately. The threat of being caught doubles his shadow. Every day comrades disappear, are tortured, or shot. He goes from one precarious refuge to another, without hearth or home, hunted, hidden, a phantom of himself.

And Gerbier continued:

— But he is never alone. He feels around him the faith and tenderness of a whole enslaved people. He finds his accomplices, he finds friends in the fields and in the factories. In the suburbs and in the castles, among gendarmes, railroad workers, smugglers, merchants and priests. Among old notaries and with young girls. The poorest sharing his meager ration of bread with him. He who did not even have the right to enter a bakery, because he fights for all the harvests of France.

So spoke Gerbier. And Legrain on his burning pallet, in the stifling darkness, discovered a wholly new and enchanted country, peopled with countless unarmed fighters, a homeland of sacred friends — more beautiful than any country that ever existed on earth. The resistance was this country.

———

One morning, while going to work, Legrain suddenly asked:

— Monsieur Gerbier, are you a leader in the resistance?

Gerbier considered Legrain's burning & ravaged young face with almost cruel attention. He saw boundless loyalty and devotion in it.

— I was in the headquarters of a movement, he said. No one here knows. I came from Paris, but I was arrested in Toulouse on a denunciation, I think. But without proof. They didn't even dare judge me. So they sent me here.

— For how long? asked Legrain.

Gerbier shrugged his shoulders & smiled.

— For as long as they please, come on, he said. You know that better than anyone.

Legrain stopped and stared at the ground. Then he said in a stifled but very firm voice:

— Monsieur Gerbier, we need you to get out of here.

Legrain paused, then looked up and said:

— They need you outside.

Since Gerbier didn't respond, Legrain continued:

— I have an idea… and I've had it for a long time… I'll tell you about it tonight.

They parted. Gerbier bought cigarettes from a guard who served as his procurer. He made the rounds of the field.

He had his usual smile. Yet he reached the goal he had pursued through the stories & images with which he had patiently intoxicated Legrain.

———————

— I'll tell you my idea, whispered Legrain, when he was assured that the colonel, the traveling salesman, and the pharmacist were fast asleep.

Legrain composed himself & searched for words. Then he said:

— What prevents escape? There are two things — the barbed wire and the patrols. As for the barbed wire, the ground is not level everywhere, and there are places where a man as slender as you are, Monsieur Gerbier, may squeeze under, though he might gash himself a bit.

— I know all those places, said Gerbier.

— So much for the barbed wire, said Legrain. The patrols remain. How many minutes do you need to run as far as the patrol road, slip away, and lose yourself in the woods?

— Twelve … fifteen at most, said Gerbier.

— Eh, well, I can ensure that the guards will be blind for longer than that, said Legrain.

— I think so, Gerbier said quietly. It's not difficult for a skilled electrician to arrange a power failure in advance.

— You thought of it, murmured Legrain. And you never said a word to me.

— I can command or obey. I don't know how to ask, said Gerbier. I was waiting for it to come from you.

Gerbier leaned on one elbow as if trying to discern his companion's face through the dark. And he said:

— I've often wondered why, having this means at your disposal, you haven't benefitted from it.

Legrain had a coughing fit before answering.

— In the beginning, I spoke about it with Armel. He wasn't of the mind. He resigned himself too easily, perhaps. But in a way it was true what he said. With our blousons and no papers, no ration card, we wouldn't have got far. Then Armel fell ill. I couldn't leave him. And myself, I wasn't managing well. For you it's different. With your friends in the resistance …

— I've already established contact through the guard who sells me cigarettes, said Gerbier.

He added without transition:

— In a week, two at the latest, we can leave.

There was a silence. And Legrain's heart thumped so strongly against his emaciated ribs that Gerbier could hear it beating. The young man muttered:

— Is that what you promised, *us*, Monsieur Gerbier?

— But obviously, said Gerbier. What then were you thinking?

— I believed at times that you'd take me with you. But I dared not be sure, said Legrain.

Gerbier asked slowly and emphasized each word:

— So you had accepted the idea of preparing my escape while staying here?

— The thing was heard like that with me, said Legrain.

— And you would've done it?

— We need you, Monsieur Gerbier, in the resistance.

For some minutes Gerbier had longed to smoke. Yet he waited before lighting a cigarette. He hated to reveal the least emotion on his face.

———

When beginning his game of dominœs, Colonel Jarret du Plessis made this remark to his companions:

— The little communist looks like he just awoke. Every time he goes to work he croons.

— It's spring, assured the traveling salesman.

— It's rather that you get used to everything, sighed the pharmacist. Him just like the others, the poor kid.

The three men had no hostility against Legrain. On the contrary his age, his misfortune, his physical condition softened their natural bonhomie. They had offered to keep watch of Armel turn by turn. But Legrain, jealous of his friend, had declined their services. When they received packages with food from outside, they always wanted to give Legrain a share. But, knowing he had no chance of reciprocating those courtesies, Legrain was stubborn in his refusal without appeal. Gradually, because of that rough disposition, the domino players had come to forget the existence of the young man. His change in attitude made them notice him again. One evening when the pharmacist shared some chocolate bars he had received from his family, Legrain reached out.

— Bravo! exclaimed Colonel du Plessis. The little communist is getting domesticated.

The Colonel turned toward Gerbier and said:

— This is your influence, Monsieur, & I congratulate you.

— I believe more that it's the chocolate, said Gerbier.

A few hours later, when they were the only ones still awake, Gerbier said to Legrain:

— You chose a bad time to display your gluttony.

— I thought ... I thought I'd be able to send him something in return soon, the young man murmured.

— They may have had the same thought. We should never believe people to be stupider than ourselves, said Gerbier.

They were silent. After a few moments Legrain asked humbly:

— Are you angry with me, Monsieur Gerbier?

— But no, it's finished, said Gerbier.

— Then you'll tell me what'll happen after the power failure? asked Legrain.

— I already explained the details yesterday, and the day before, said Gerbier.

— If you can say it again, said Legrain, because I cannot believe it, and I won't sleep ... So really, there'll be a car?

— A gazogène, said Gerbier. And I think Guillaume will be at the wheel.

— The former sergeant of the Foreign Legion? The hard one? The one they also call the Bison? Legrain whispered.

— There'll be civilian clothes in the car, continued Gerbier. They'll take us to a presbytery. Then we'll see.

— And friends of the resistance will give us false papers? asked Legrain.

— And ration cards.

— And you'll introduce me to communists, Monsieur Gerbier? And I'll work with them for the resistance?

— I promise you.

— But we'll continue to see one another, you and me, Monsieur Gerbier?

— If you're a liaison agent.

— That's what I want to be, said Legrain.

And during the nights that followed, Legrain asked each time.

— Tell me of Guillaume, the Bison, Monsieur Gerbier, and about everything, please.

———

Gerbier found a sheet of thin paper inside the pack of cigarettes that he'd bought. He went to the latrine, carefully read the message, then burned it. Next, he made a round of the barbed wire, as he usually did. At the end of the afternoon, he said to Legrain:

— Everything's in order. We leave Saturday.

— In four days, stammered Legrain.

The blood completely left his gaunt cheeks then returned with strength, then left them again. Legrain leaned against Gerbier saying:

— Excuse me … my head's spinning. It's happiness.

Legrain let himself fall gently against the ground. Gerbier took note that the last week had terribly taxed the young man. His face had shrunk & his eyes had grown larger.

His nose was as thin as a fishbone. One saw much more of his Adam's apple.

— You need to calm yourself, and control your emotions, said Gerbier, with severity, and, before Saturday, you have to regain your strength. There are still five kilometers to walk. You'll take my soup at lunch, you hear.

— I will do it, Monsieur Gerbier.

— And you don't sleep enough. Tomorrow you'll ask for tablets at the infirmary.

— I will, Monsieur Gerbier.

Legrain left the barrack earlier than usual and Gerbier accompanied him up until the doorstep.

— Only three more nights here, and it's the Bison's car, said Legrain.

Off he ran. Gerbier followed him with his eyes & thought: "He's young, he'll last."

At lunch, Gerbier gave his mess tin to Legrain. But he shook his head.

— I well know it was agreed upon, but I can't, it twists my heart, he said.

— Then take my bread, said Gerbier, you can eat it while working.

Legrain shoved the blackish slice into the pocket of his blouson. His gesture was languid, burdened. His face dazed.

— You have a morose air, remarked Gerbier.

Legrain didn't answer and walked in the direction of the power station. That evening he didn't ask Gerbier to talk to him about the Bison & the other wonders.

— You took your tablet? Gerbier asked.

— I took it. I'll fall asleep in no time, I think, said Legrain.

On Thursday his conduct was even more unusual. He didn't eat breakfast, and, in the barrack, while waiting for nightfall, he watched the game of dominœs instead of talking with Gerbier. He seemed to sink into sleep in one fell swoop.

On Friday, Legrain had an absurd argument with the pharmacist and accused him of being a dirty bourgeois. Gerbier said nothing at the moment, but, in the darkness and the silence, he roughly grabbed Legrain's arm as he seemed to already be sleeping and asked:

— What's the point?

— But ... nothing, Monsieur Gerbier, said Legrain.

— I beg you to answer, said Gerbier. You've no more confidence? Your nerves frazzled? I give you my word that on my part everything will be taken care of.

— I know, Monsieur Gerbier.

— And on your end?

— The work will be clean, I can assure you.

— Then what is it?

— I don't know, Monsieur Gerbier, really ... Headache. The heart's knotted up ...

Gerbier's eyes narrowed as they did in daylight when he wanted to break through the secret of a face. But they were powerless in the dark.

—You must've taken too many tablets, Gerbier finally said.

— Surely, Monsieur Gerbier, said Legrain.

— You'll feel better tomorrow, Gerbier resumed, when you see the car with the Bison.

— The Bison, repeated Legrain.

But he went no further.

Thereafter, Gerbier frequently recalled the unconscious and frightful cruelty of this dialogue in the night.

———

Saturday morning, in the midst of his usual walk, Gerbier passed by the power station where, since the removal of the old Austrian engineer, Legrain worked alone. Gerbier saw with satisfaction that Legrain was calm.

— Everything's ready, said the young man.

Gerbier examined Legrain's work. The clocklike mechanism that would trigger the short circuit was designed with intelligence & consummate skill. The current will be broken at the desired time.

— And it'll be calm, assured Legrain, it'll take at least forty minutes for the fools on the night shift to repair it.

— No one could have done better than you. It's as if we're as good as out, said Gerbier.

— Thank you, Monsieur Gerbier, murmured the young man.

His eyes were very bright.

———

The Colonel, the pharmacist, & the traveling salesman were finishing their game of dominœs by the last light of day. The grey mist of twilight accrued on the field. But a belt of hard and fixed light imprisoned dusk within the camp. The patrol road between the webs of metal brambles was violently illuminated. Behind this belt and by contrast it was already night. In front of their barrack, Gerbier and Legrain silently regarded the glimmering barbed wire. From time to time, Gerbier would reach into the bottom of his pocket to touch the tool that Legrain had brought from the workshop to spring the locks. A guard in a beret shouted:

— Roll call.

Gerbier and Legrain returned. The guard counted the occupants of the barrack and shut the doors. It was dark once again. Each fumbled for his straw mattress. From time to time, the Colonel, the traveling salesman, & the pharmacist exchanged words that became increasingly desultory. Gerbier and Legrain were silent. Their cellmates dozed off with their usual sighs. Gerbier and Legrain were silent.

Gerbier was pleased with Legrain's silence. He had feared that he'd suffer an excess of agitation during this wait. The mechanism Legrain rigged up would go off at midnight. They still had about an hour. Gerbier smoked several cigarettes then went to the door & jimmied the lock without making any noise. He gave the door a push. He saw the brutal light that encircled the field. Gerbier returned to his straw mattress and gave notice.

— You be ready, Roger, it won't be much longer.

Then, once again, Gerbier heard the movements of Legrain's heart.

— Monsieur Gerbier, the young man murmured with difficulty, I must tell you something.

He caught his breath, with difficulty.

— I'm not leaving, he said.

In spite of all his self-control, Gerbier was on the verge of raising his voice in an imprudent way. But he mastered himself and spoke at the usual pitch of these conversations in the shadows.

— Are you scared? he asked softly.

— Oh! Monsieur Gerbier, Legrain moaned.

And Gerbier felt sure that Legrain was inaccessible to fear. As sure as if he could've seen his face.

— You believe that you're too tired to make the road? said Gerbier. I'll carry you if necessary.

— I would've made it. I would've made it even much farther, said Legrain.

And Gerbier felt that that was true.

— I'll explain to you, Monsieur Gerbier, just don't talk to me, Legrain said. I need to do it quickly, and that's quite difficult.

Legrain's lungs wheezed. He coughed and resumed:

— When I went to get the sleeping pills as you had commanded me, I saw the doctor. He's nice, the doctor. He's an old man who understands. He set Armel and me up here, because at least it's not raining through the roof and the floor stays dry. He couldn't do anything else. This is to tell you that one can talk to him. But he didn't find me well. He auscultated me. I didn't understand everything of what he told me … But anyway enough to know that I'd lost a lung and the other could be lost. He sighed hard to see me still imprisoned & with no hope of escape. So I asked him what would happen if I got out. Then he told me that with two years in a sanatorium, I could be well again. Otherwise, I'm good for nothing. I left his place stunned. You saw me … I was thinking all the time about what you had told me of the life of the resistance. It took me till this morning to realize that I can't go.

Gerbier believed himself to be very hard. And he was. He didn't believe in acting without thinking. And he did it. He had inflamed Legrain with his stories so as to have a trustworthy accomplice. Yet it was without reflection, without calculation, and seized by an unknown contraction, he said:

— I won't leave you. I have the financial means and I'll find others; you'll be safe, cared for. You'll have the time you need to recuperate.

— That wasn't why I was leaving, Monsieur Gerbier, said the calm voice of the invisible young man. I wanted to be a liaison agent. I don't want to take ration cards from the comrades for my poor health. I don't want to encumber the resistance. You've shown me very well what it is.

Gerbier felt physically unable to respond, and Legrain continued:

— But all the same, I'm glad to know of the resistance. I won't be so unhappy. I understand life and I love it. I'm like Armel, now. I have faith.

He brightened up a bit and said in a fierce tone:

— But it's not in the other world that I expect justice, Monsieur Gerbier. Tell our friends here and on the other side of the water, tell them to hurry. I wish I had time to see the end of men with empty eyes.

He was mute, and the silence that followed, neither one nor the other, neither of them measured time. Unknowingly they were both staring at the crack of the door through which they saw the shining lights of the patrol road. They got up at the same time because that luminous thread of light suddenly snapped. The darkness of freedom had joined the imprisoned darkness. Gerbier and Legrain were at the door.

Against all prudence, against all common sense, Gerbier spoke again:

— They'll discover the sabotage; they'll see that I escaped. They'll realize everything. They'll think of you.

— What more can they do to me? murmured Legrain.

Gerbier was still not leaving.

— On the contrary, I'll be useful to you, said the young man. They'll come to me to fix things. I'll get out so fast that they won't see your empty straw mattress & I'll tangle them up for a good half hour. You'll be far away with the Bison.

Gerbier crossed the threshold.

— Think over it one last time, he said, almost pleading.

— I was never the kind to be a burden to anyone, said Legrain. It's not going to begin with the resistance.

Gerbier slipped between the doors without looking back & headed straight for the gap in the barbed wire. He'd studied it a hundred times & he'd counted a hundred times the steps needed to reach this spot.

Legrain carefully closed the door, went toward his pallet, bit the canvas on the straw mattress & lay there, very somber.

2

THE EXECUTION

A note from the organization which Paul Dounat (who was now called Vincent Henry) belonged to had instructed him to be in Marseille toward the middle of the afternoon & to wait in front of the Église des Réformés for a comrade whom he knew well. Dounat had been at the appointed place for a few minutes when a gazogène car drove by him and stopped about thirty meters beyond. A short-statured man stepped out. He wore a bowler hat, a dark maroon overcoat, and his shoulders lunged heavily as he walked. This man whom Dounat had never met went straight to him and said, showing a *Sûreté* card:

— Police, your papers.

Dounat obeyed. His false identity documents were in perfect order. The man in the bowler hat said with more amenity:

— I see that you are in order, Monsieur. All the same, I shall ask you to accompany me to our offices. A simple verification.

Dounat bowed. He did not fear the verification.

The driver was standing near the running board of the car. He was massive and had the crushed nose of a boxer. He opened the door and pushed Dounat inside with a single movement. The man in the bowler hat followed closely on Dounat's heels. The car started off swiftly up the slope. Ensconced in the corner of the seat, with his head held back so that he could not be seen from outside, Dounat saw André Roussel, who also bore the name of Philippe Gerbier and who had let his mustache grow. All of Dounat's blood suddenly rushed to his heart and he collapsed on the folding seat like a man disjointed.

The fake policeman wiped his bald-shaped tonsure, considered his hat with disgust, and grumbled:

— Dirty work.

— Félix, you good and well hate bowlers, but you must submit to it all the same, Gerbier said absent-mindedly.

— I know that, Félix grumbled, but only when we stop.

Dounat thought: "It's then that they'll kill me."

He formulated this thought with indifference. He was no longer afraid. The first shock had exhausted all living sensation in him. As always, and when he no longer had any choice, he resigned himself to the worst with docility and a strange ease. He would have wanted only to drink something strong. His veins seemed all hollow to him.

— Look at him, Félix said to Gerbier. It's damn well him who sold out you and Zephyr and the radio operator.

Gerbier agreed with a slight movement of his eyelids. He didn't want to talk. He didn't want to think. Everything was made obvious by Dounat's very attitude: treason, and the inner mechanism of this treason. Dounat had been brought into the resistance by his mistress. She could stimulate him so well. He had proved useful, intelligent, and courageous. When Françoise was arrested, he continued to act out of torpidity. Taken in turn, but quickly released, he became a tool of the police.

"We should've stopped using him when Françoise disappeared, said Gerbier. That was a mistake. But we have so few people and so many missions to cover."

Gerbier lit a cigarette. Through the smoke Dounat appeared to him even more vague, more inconsistent than usual. Good family, good manners ... pleasing features ... A small mole in the middle of his upper lip made his mouth, which was beautiful and tender, more prominent. The face was smooth, without pronounced edges, and ended with an indeterminate, slightly fat chin.

"Laziness manifested in the will," thought Gerbier distractedly. "He needs someone who decides in his place. Françoise, the police, & now us ... For the action, denouncement, death."

Gerbier said in a loud voice:

— I believe, Paul, that it's useless to give you our proof & to ask you questions.

Dounat didn't even raise his head. Gerbier continued smoking. He experienced the kind of boredom that a tedious and necessary formality provokes. He began to think of everything that he had to do afterwards. His report, consign two instructors ... write encrypted messages for London ...

the meeting with the big boss who was coming from Paris … choose the C. P. for the next day.

— Can we not hurry? Gerbier asked Félix.

— I don't believe so, said Félix. The Bison knows his job like no one else. He drives as fast as anyone can without attracting attention.

Dounat, his chin resting in one hand, looked toward the coast.

— I'm in a hurry myself, continued Félix. I have that old position I have to review. I have to change the handlebars on a bike for a liaison agent. And then there's the parachute drop tonight.

— The new false papers? Gerbier asked.

— I have them on me, said Félix. I give them to you now?

Gerbier nodded his head.

Dounat understood perfectly that if the two men spoke with such freedom in his presence, then they felt certain of his silence, of his eternal silence. They were already concerned with the moment — and it was close — when he would be effaced from the human order. But this condemnation left Dounat without anxiety or turmoil. For him, likewise, his death was an accepted fact. It belonged somehow to the past. The present alone had a value and a meaning. And now that the car had overtaken the peak of the Old Port, the present was entirely formed, and with a prodigious intensity, of that expanse of blue water, of those islets, jagged like ancient galleys, of those pure & arid hills, the color of light sand which seemed to uphold the sky on the other side of the gulf.

Suddenly, as the car passed before Hotel de la Corniche, which Dounat recognized, Françoise's face united and absorbed all the scattered features of this magnificence. She was standing at the edge of the terrace that jutted over the sea.

She was wearing a summer dress tied around her neck that left her arms bare. She carried the light and warmth of the day in the generous substance of her face. Dounat caressed her beautiful neck with a light & familiar movement; she turned her head slightly, and Dounat saw her throat, her shoulders, her swelling chest expanding, like those plants that suddenly ripen. And Françoise kissed him on the mole he had in the middle of his upper lip.

Unconsciously, Dounat touched that little brown spot. Unconsciously, too, Gerbier touched the mustache that he wore, still rough, since his escape from Camp L.... Félix considered his bowler hat with disgust.

A bend in the road concealed the hotel from Dounat's sight. The image of Françoise's thrown-back head disappeared. That didn't astonish Dounat. Those games belonged to another age of the world. Clandestine life, then, had not yet begun.

Félix struck the edge of his bowler hat against the glass that separated him from the driver. Then he crammed the bowler to the top of his bald head. The car stopped. Dounat ceased contemplating the sea and turned toward the other side of the boulevard. There was a hillside with a very swift slope that was covered with a cluster of little houses & small and peaceful villas that were both modest and miserable.

The car was idling at the bottom of a lane without asphalt or pavement that rose up like a mountain path between those low houses and those sad little gardens.

The driver lowered the window positioned behind him and said to Gerbier:

— The gazo will have a hard time of it on that steep slope.

— And it'll make a great noise ... everybody will be at their windows, said Félix.

Gerbier focused his eyes narrowly on Dounat's profile. The latter, expressionless, was again facing the sea.

— We'll go by foot, said Gerbier.

— I'll go with you then, said the driver.

He had the hoarse voice of a man who smoked too much, drank too much, and who was taken to shouting orders for a long time. His tanned and massive face almost completely filled up the window frame.

Gerbier looked at Dounat once more and said:

— It's not worth the trouble, Guillaume.

— Really not, said Félix.

The driver in turn looked at Dounat & grumbled:

— I agree with you.

Gerbier waited for a groaning tram and passengers crowding the steps to pass. Then he opened the door. Félix took one of Dounat's arms and Gerbier took the other.

— I'll get the crates and I'll be back at night, for the body, said the driver as he was about to roll off.

Dounat climbed the steep alley, sandwiched between Félix and Gerbier, as if between two friends, and he thought of how the communists sometimes disposed of their traitors. At night, they would lure the man to the seaside, poleax him, undress him, roll him up in trellis wire, and throw him into the water. Crabs would entirely devour the body through the mesh. Françoise had been with Dounat the night he had heard this story. A fierce burst of passion inflamed her face, which was ordinarily so sweet and gay. "I'd like to take part in such an operation," said Françoise. "There is no death vile enough for people who sell out their comrades." Dounat remembered that paroxysm and also that the neck of his mistress had flushed a deep pink, and he was docile as Gerbier and Félix led him up the high dusty alley.

On the doorsteps you could sometimes see a woman in a black skirt, with disheveled hair, lazily shaking a rug. Children were playing in squalid little gardens. A man leaning against a fence was scratching his bare ankles above his slippers as he watched the three bystanders. At each of those encounters, Félix jabbed the revolver that he held firmly grasped in his pocket and snarled into Dounat's ear:

— One word and I'll slaughter you in a second.

But in the arm that he held, Gerbier felt only softness, obedience. He experienced anew a feeling of profound boredom.

They finally turned into a narrow impasse, flanked by blind walls, and obstructed at the end by two identical cottages flush one against the other. The shutters were raised in the one to the left.

— *My God*, said Félix, stopping brutally.

His frank & round face was totally crippled.

— Ours, he said to Gerbier, it's the cottage on the right with the closed shutters.

Félix swore again.

— The other day, when we rented it, the nearby shack was empty, he continued.

— It's obviously irritating, but more reason not to get noticed, said Gerbier. Come on.

The three men were soon at the end of the impasse. Then the door of the right cottage seemed to open on its own and they went inside. The boy who was standing behind the door immediately pushed it closed, shut the wicket flap, gave a turn of the key. All his movements were made silently. But in their haste and cadence was an evil, nervous tension. And Gerbier had further evidence of this when he heard a jerky whisper.

— The back room … go then to the back room …

Félix pushed Dounat by the neck and followed him.

— It's him … the traitor … who's got to be … asked the boy who welcomed the group in a barely audible voice.

— It's him, said Gerbier.

— And you're the boss?

— I'm in charge of this assignment, said Gerbier.

They each went to the back room in turn. The shutters were drawn, and, after the glare of daylight, the darkness seemed intense at first. But enough light entered through the badly joined shutters so that they could, in a few moments, see clearly. Then Gerbier could make out plaster flakes that quivered on the ceiling, moisture stains on the walls, two mismatched chairs, and directly on the floor, a mattress covered with a quilt. And he could examine the comrade chosen by Félix to help with Dounat's execution. He was a tall, upright young man, lean, modestly dressed, with a sharp-featured & sensitive face. He had slightly bulging, scintillating eyes.

Félix pointed his bowler hat in the direction of the young man and said to Gerbier:

— There's Claude Lemasque.

Gerbier smiled halfway. He knew that the nicknames often revealed a character element when the person chose it himself. This one had come to the resistance with the religion of secret societies.

— He's been crying for a long time for a hard stint, added Félix.

Lemasque hurriedly told Gerbier:

— I came here more than an hour ago to put everything in order. That's when I saw the disaster next door. They got here this morning, or during the night at the earliest. Last night I passed through here and there was nobody. When I saw the open shutters, I ran to call Félix, but he was already on his way. There was nothing to do, was there?

— Absolutely nothing, I assure you, absolutely nothing, said Gerbier, with all the slowness and all the evenness of tone that he could put in a few words.

This kid spoke too much, spoke too low, spoke too fast.

— The place is good, said Gerbier, it'll work out.

— We can go on to the interrogation if you want, said Lemasque. Everything is ready up there in the attic. It's a bit like a court. I put some chairs, a table, some paper.

Gerbier half-smiled *&* said:

— This isn't a trial.

— This is it, Félix said impatiently.

He had pulled from his pocket the butt of a revolver that he had continually been fingering. The metal shone in the semi-darkness. Lemasque glanced toward Dounat for the first time. He was leaning against a wall and looking at no one.

The men who surrounded him continued to lack volume and reality. But things were armed with a power he had never known them to have. The flaking ceiling, the moldy walls, and the furniture seemed to be waiting, observing and understanding. The objects had relief, substance, and a density of life that Dounat hadn't. However, his eyes had finally settled on a drab, reddish-brown quilt. Dounat recognized it. In doubtful hotels, in poor transient houses, where between missions, he had been lucky enough to meet Françoise, Dounat had always seen that quilt. That again belonged to another age of this world. Refinements no longer had any place in it. The hazards, the perils of covert action, gave their form and their color to love. Françoise would sit down on the red quilt, fix her hair, and in a choked and happy voice, recount the events of her days and nights. She loved this work, she loved the leaders, she loved the comrades, she loved France. And Dounat felt that she physically carried this passion over to him. So he too loved the resistance. He was no longer harassed, he was not anxious about being homeless and nameless. He was no longer a lawless, hunted, lost man. Under the red quilt he would press against Françoise's shoulders and breasts. This warm, exalted, courageous body became a sort of wonderful lair, a place of asylum. An extraordinary starry safety enveloped pleasure.

— Well? asked Félix, pulling out his revolver.

— It's impossible … impossible … said Lemasque. I was here before you. You can hear everything … Hold on …

In the neighboring cottage a little girl began to sing a wispy and monotonous melody. The song seemed to rise from the same room.

— These aren't walls, they're cigarette paper, said Lemasque with fury.

Félix put his revolver in his pocket & swore.

— Are those damned Englishmen ever going to send us the silencers we asked for?

— Come with me, said Gerbier. We'll see if there's not a more suitable spot.

Gerbier and Félix left the room. Lemasque swiftly placed himself in front of the door as if Dounat had wanted to escape. But Dounat didn't move.

As Lemasque had anticipated, nothing was happening. He had prepared himself with profound exaltation for an act that would be terrible but full of solemnity. Three men would sit there: a leader of the organization, Félix, and himself. Before them the traitor would defend his life with lies punctuated by desperate screams. They would entangle him in contradictions. And Lemasque would kill him, proud to pierce a criminal's heart. In place of this fierce justice … the song of a little girl, the steps of his accomplices resonating upstairs, and before him this man with light auburn hair, young, with a sad, docile face, with his mole in the center of his lip and who kept obstinately staring at a red quilt.

In truth, Dounat no longer saw the quilt. What he now saw was Françoise, naked, in the midst of the police who were tormenting her. Dounat pressed himself more & more against the wall. He felt near to fainting. But it wasn't only terror in the depth of his weakness.

The little girl continued to sing. Her quavering and fragile voice communicated an unbearable anxiety to Lemasque's nerves.

— How could you? he suddenly asked Dounat.

Dounat raised his head mechanically. Lemasque could not guess the nature of the images that gave Dounat's eyes their humble, ashamed, & troubled expression. But he saw in them such deep human misery that he felt like screaming.

Gerbier and Félix reappeared.

— Nothing doing, said the latter. The basement is connected to the neighboring one and the attic carries more sound than here.

— We must do something though; we've got to, murmured Lemasque, whose thin hands were beginning to flutter with impatience.

Félix clenched his fists and said:

— We need a solid knife. The Bison always has one on him.

— A knife? murmured Lemasque. A knife … You're not seriously thinking of that.

Félix's frank, round face became very red.

— Do you believe that it's for fun, imbecile? Félix said in an almost menacing tone.

— If you try it, I'll prevent it, whispered Lemasque.

— And I'll smash your fucking teeth, said Félix.

Gerbier smiled his half-smile.

— Look in the dining room and in the kitchen to see if you find something that we could use, he told Félix.

Lemasque feverishly approached Gerbier & said in his ear:

— It's impossible, think, I beg you. It's murder.

— In any case, we're here to kill, said Gerbier. You agree?

— I ... I agree ... Lemasque stammered. But not like this ... We must ...

— How it's done, I know, I know, said Gerbier.

Lemasque was not accustomed to that half-smile.

— I'm not afraid, I swear, he said.

— I know, I know ... It's quite another thing, said Gerbier.

— I'm doing this for the first time, you understand, replied Lemasque.

— For us too, it's the first time, said Gerbier. I guess that it shows.

He looked at Dounat, who recovered a bit. His weakness had disappeared, and so had the image of Françoise. The last age of the world had come.

The door opened.

—For fuck's sake, said Félix, empty-handed.

He looked very tired and his eyes wandered to every part of the room, but avoided the place where Dounat stood.

— I thought, Félix replied silently, I thought that maybe in leaving it until the night, until the arrival of the Bison, it'd be better.

— No, said Gerbier, we're all very busy, and then I need to report to the boss that the case is finished.

— In the name of God, in the name of God, we can't just smash his skull with a rifle butt, said Félix.

At that moment Dounat made his first spontaneous movement. He batted his arms feebly and placed his open palms over his face. Gerbier realized to what extent Dounat feared physical suffering.

"Much more than death," thought Gerbier. "That's the way the police were able to force him to betray."

Gerbier said to Félix:

— Gag him.

When Félix had stuffed his thick plaid handkerchief into Dounat's mouth and Dounat had fallen on the mattress, Gerbier said neatly:

— Strangle him.

— With … our hands? … Félix asked.

— No, Gerbier said, there's a towel in the kitchen that'll do just fine.

Lemasque began to pace the room. He didn't notice that he was pulling so hard on his fingers that the joints cracked. Suddenly he boxed his ears. The little girl in the neighboring house was beginning to sing again. His facial expression was such that Gerbier was afraid he was going to suffer a nervous breakdown. He went up to Lemasque and brutally knocked his hands down.

— No mishaps, I beg you, said Gerbier. Dounat has got to die. That's what you came here for and you will help us. One of our radio operators was shot because of him. A comrade is dying in Germany — is that not sufficient for you?

The young man wanted to speak. Gerbier didn't give him a chance.

— You're employed at the Town Hall, I know, and also as a reserve officer. And it isn't your job to choke a defenseless man. But Félix is a mechanic and I'm an engineer. Only, in truth, you and Félix and me, we're nothing more than men of the resistance. And that changes everything. Would you have thought before that you would enjoy making fake tickets, fake stamps, forged documents, that you would be proud of being a forger? You asked to do something more difficult. You are servants. Don't complain.

Félix had returned without making a noise and he was listening.

— We have a specialist for executions, continued Gerbier. But he isn't free today. And all the better. Everyone must have his share of harder tasks. We need to learn. It isn't vengeance. It isn't even justice. It's a necessity. We don't have a prison to protect us from dangerous people.

— That's right, said Félix. I'm glad I heard you.

His frank, round face had an implacable sort of serenity. He carefully stretched the long, stiff towel that he'd brought from the kitchen. Lemasque was still trembling. But his tremor was weakening like the end of a fever spell.

— Take Dounat to that chair, said Gerbier. Félix, if you stand behind him, I'll hold his arms and Lemasque will hold his knees.

Dounat didn't resist.

And vaguely astonished to see that everything unfolded with such ease — especially internally —, Gerbier came up behind the back of the chair, above which Dounat's head protruded. But when seizing his shoulders, Gerbier hesitated. He had just noticed, on Dounat's neck, a little below the ear, a mole like the one he had on his upper lip. Because of this little spot, the flesh which here surrounded it seemed more alive, more tender, more vulnerable, like some remnant of childhood. And Gerbier felt that this flesh was barely capable of enduring torture. Through this flesh, the traitor Dounat became innocent. The Bison could endure torture. And Félix. And Gerbier himself. But not Dounat, & doubtless not the young man who, clinging to the knees of the condemned, breathed like a death rattle.

Opposite Gerbier, Félix was waiting for the leader to make a sign. But Gerbier's arms were so heavy that he could not bring them to Dounat's shoulders.

"Without a doubt, Félix, at this moment, has a more frightful look on his face than this wretch," thought Gerbier.

Then he thought of bonhomie, of fidelity, of Félix's courage, of his wife, of his little sickly and underfed boy, of all that Félix had done for the resistance. Not to kill Dounat was to kill Félix. Dounat alive would betray Félix. This was also inscribed in the little brown spot and too tender flesh of his neck. Gerbier suddenly had the strength to lift his arms. It wasn't Dounat's fault if he was going to die and it wasn't the fault of those who were killing him. The sole eternal culprit was the enemy who imposed on the French the fatality of horror.

Gerbier's hands fell on Dounat's shoulders. At the same time Gerbier said in his ear:

— I swear to you, my poor old man, you won't feel any pain.

The rolled dishrag destroyed the feeble neck. Félix pulled savagely at both ends. Gerbier felt the life run very fast from the arms he was holding. It seemed to him that their convulsions passed into his own body. Each of them accumulated in Gerbier a new force of hatred against the German and his minions.

Gerbier carried Dounat's body to the mattress and covered it with the red quilt.

He went to the window. Through the slits in the shutters, he saw an empty lot. The spot was well chosen.

Félix put on his bowler hat. His short and strong legs were a bit unsteady.

— We're going? he asked in a hoarse voice.

— In a moment, said Gerbier.

Lemasque approached Gerbier. His sharp, nervous face was covered with sweat.

— I didn't believe, he said, that we could do so much for the resistance.

He began to weep silently.

— Me neither, said Gerbier.

He cast a quick glance at the red quilt and said with kindness to Lemasque:

— You must always have cyanide pills on you. And if you
get caught, you take them yourself, old man.

3

LEAVING FOR GIBRALTAR

I

Jean-François was walking very quickly along the Promenade des Anglais, although it was too early to go to a fashionable bar to join a few comrades who met there every day, refugees from Paris like himself who were as idle as him. Jean-François was walking quickly because of the sun, the sea breaking on the pebbles, and because of his youth. Before arriving at Place Masséna, Jean-François stopped in front of a luxury shirt shop. There was a display case of beautiful silk bathrobes that one could buy without ration tickets. Jean-François had no need of a bathrobe. However, he entered the store. He had to do something. The salesman smiled because everyone smiled at Jean-François, who was handsome, strong, simple, and who had blue eyes free of reservation. And because the salesman smiled, Jean-François bought two bathrobes. He left, thought himself very foolish, and laughed all alone. At that moment, he saw a man in a leather overcoat with a small but powerful torso and neck, tearing along more than walking, rolling his shoulders formidably.

— Félix, shouted Jean-François, with all his strength. Félix la Tonsure!

The man turned round with a hard and swift movement, recognized Jean-François, and just then smiled. They had served in the same *Corps Franc* during the war.

— You haven't changed, baby, said Félix, forever young & beautiful.

— And you, let's see … said Jean-François.

He wanted to lift Félix la Tonsure's fedora to joke about the bald spot that gave him his nickname. The other stopped him.

— I'm afraid of drafts, he said curtly.

— By what chance are you here in Nice? And your garage in Levallois? asked Jean-François.

— The Fritzes wanted me to work on their repairs. So you can imagine I did them in, said Félix.

His full and vibrant face had this abstract expression, which Jean-François had seen in him on ambush or on patrol. He was a courageous man, direct, on the up and up, as Jean-François liked men to be.

— Let's have a drink, he said.

But Félix refused. They would drink after. First he wanted to speak to Jean-François.

They went down a quieter street.

— What are you doing in civilian life now? asked Félix.

— But nothing at all, said Jean-François.

— And against the Krauts?

— But … nothing either, said Jean-François, more slowly.

— Why?

— I don't know … said Jean-François. How manage it? Alone, we can do nothing … and around me, no one …

— Eh, well, I've a job for you, lazybones, said Félix. It'll suit you better than a flower. Secret papers to carry discreetly, weapons to conceal, and instructions to give to stupefied little guys on how to outsmart the pigs and the Gestapo. A real honest grind like in the *Corps Franc*. The beautiful life.

— The beautiful life, repeated Jean-François.

The one he'd been leading had become unbearable all of a sudden.

— You'll have to get up early, said Félix, and spend nights on the road without knowing a thing, without trying to understand.

— I love movement and I'm not curious, you know that, said Jean-François.

Félix la Tonsure rested his eyes for a moment on his companion's athletic shoulders, on his handsome, resolute, and clear face.

— Guys who can attack like you, we need 'em, Félix said. I haven't wasted my day.

They took a few steps in silence, pleased with one another. Then Félix went on:

— Come see me tomorrow in Marseille. I've got a little bike shop there. I feed my kids this way and I have a cover. I'll give you the address.

Jean-François reached into his pocket for a notebook.

— None of that, my man, none of that! exclaimed Félix.

Nothing written, ever. Everything by heart, everything in your head.

Félix stared fixedly at Jean-François and continued:

— And you don't say so much as a word. Not a word to anyone. Understand?

— I'm not crazy, said Jean-François.

— Everyone says the same thing, Félix remarked. And then you've got a wife ...

Jean-François shrugged his shoulders.

— Or relatives you never keep anything from, Félix went on.

— My father and mother are dead and I only have one older brother who wouldn't leave Paris, said Jean-François.

He suddenly laughed and added:

— I love him, but there's no danger of my confiding anything to him. He's a baby.

Félix regarded Jean-François' very fresh face and laughed in turn.

— And you're a connoisseur, said Félix.

He gave his address to Jean-François and they entered the first café they found. It was, by chance, a day when they had alcohol.

II

This life was truly a life made for Jean-François. All the elements that could please him were herein combined: violent physical exercise, the risk and the joy of slipping through the cracks, camaraderie, obedience to a crew leader whom he loved. Others took care of thinking and of orders. He had only the fun. He was racing, by bicycle, along the beautiful red roads of the coast. He was traveling by train to Toulouse, Lyon, and Savoy. He crossed into forbidden zones, despite the German customs officers and their dogs. He carried encrypted messages, explosives, weapons, transmitters. In barns, coves, basements, clearings, he taught simple, serious, and impassioned people how to use English submachine guns. He presented himself to them under a false name, and he didn't know who they were. Yet they loved one another with a tenderness and confidence that was without equal. One morning he swam several kilometers with goggles to locate a mysterious parcel, which a mysterious boat had anchored at sea. One moonlit night, he collected parachutes that dropped out of the deep sky.

Félix la Tonsure (Jean-François still only knew him via the cadres of the organization) spared his *Corps Franc* comrade neither fatigue nor danger.

— With your baby face, you'll pull anything off, he said.

That was true. And Jean-François felt it. And that complicity, that friendliness of fate, redoubled his strength, his boldness, & his pleasure.

Secret activity was a kind of sap. It absorbed more and more. More had been done and more remained to be done. The needs were immense. The determined and free men who gave their time and money were few and far between. Jean-François no longer slept two nights under the same roof.

He lived in the very heart of danger. Imperceptibly, he had become the man of the most hazardous feats. He owed it to his endurance, his skill, and his happy boldness. He had not for that penetrated further into the secrets of the organization to which he belonged. He belonged — thus with a handful of intrepid guys — solely to Félix la Tonsure. Félix received his orders from a higher superior. Beyond that was utter darkness. But the mystery didn't irritate, nor intrigue, nor even interest Jean-François. He felt neither its weight nor its poetry. He was born to move and to play. The unknown individuals to whom he was disposed, without knowing it, made his existence a constant *&* singular intensity. He was fulfilled.

III

A mission that took Jean-François to Paris showed him how completely he was formed and taken by the clandestine life.

When he got off the train at Gare de Lyon, he was carrying a suitcase that contained an English radio transmitter, parachuted in a few days earlier in a central department. A man caught with such baggage was fated to be tortured to death.

Presently, that morning, Gestapo agents and the *Feldgendarmerie* were inspecting all luggage at the station exit.

Jean-François had no time to think. Nearby him a child with big knees and spindly legs trotted painfully behind an elderly woman. Jean-François took the child against his chest

& at the same time handed his suitcase to a German soldier who was idly going by.

— Carry that, my old man, said Jean-François smiling. I'll never manage alone.

The German soldier looked at Jean-François, smiled in return, took the suitcase and passed without inspection. Some moments later, Jean-François was sitting in a subway station, his suitcase between his legs.

But the morning wasn't good. At the station where Jean-François got off, he found a new barrier, formed, this time, by the French police. Jean-François had to open his suitcase.

— What've you got there? asked the officer.

— As you can well see, brigadier, said Jean-François simply: a wireless device.

— So, okay, go then, said the officer.

Laughing still over these two successes, Jean-François gave the radio transmitter to a used furniture dealer on the Left Bank. The guy invited him to lunch. The day before he had just exchanged a night table for a beautiful smoked andouillette and a little butter and he was eager to share this feast with his comrade.

— Come and smell it, said the dealer.

He led Jean-François into the back of the boutique. He was gently grilling the andouillette on a cast-iron stove. Jean-François felt his nostrils stir. But he refused. He had a surprise to carry out.

Jean-François' suitcase had a wonderful lightness. And, despite a very tiring night trip, he was wonderfully refreshed.

He traversed half of Paris by foot. The swarming of enemy uniforms, the hard and sad silence of the streets, could not undermine his good mood. This morning, it was he who had won a victory.

Swinging his suitcase and whistling the march of his old regiment, Jean-François arrived at Avenue de la Muette before a little absurd and charming house, built at the end of the last century, and which belonged to his elder brother. There were beautiful paintings, innumerable books, and some precious musical instruments in this mansion. There was also, before the invasion, a quiet and refined woman, and a pugnacious little boy who had Jean-François' eyes. The mother and child had gone to the countryside when the Germans arrived and had never returned. But Jean-François' brother, he had refused to leave his house because of the paintings, musical instruments, and books.

Jean-François forbade the good old housekeeper from announcing him and quietly opened the library door. He saw his brother buried in an armchair and reading a thick volume. His face could hardly be made out because he was wearing a heavy overcoat with a collar and a wool cap pulled down over his eyes. This struck Jean-François as comical. Still excited from his brisk walk, he didn't feel how chilly the house was.

— Hey, Saint Luc, Jean-François cried.

His brother's name was simply Luc. But because of the quality of his character, his taste for the spiritual life, and his benevolence toward all men, some classmates had dubbed him Saint Luc. The name had stuck to him in the family.

— Little Jean, little Jean, said Luc, whose head barely reached Jean-François' shoulders.

The two brothers embraced each other... There was a considerable difference in age between them, but that didn't unduly impress Jean-François. He felt himself so much stronger, more practical, more resourceful than his brother.

— All the books are here, and the harpsichord and the oboe, said Jean-François. So, life is still beautiful.

— Still, still, said Luc tenderly.

Then he asked:

— But how did you come, little Jean? I hope you have an *ausweis*?[1]

— Oh! Oh! Saint Luc is no longer in the clouds. Saint Luc himself knows that it takes an *ausweis*, exclaimed Jean-François.

He laughed and Luc did too. Jean-François laughed very loud and Luc almost silently. But, although in different registers, it was the same quality of laughter.

— Yes, I have an *ausweis*, Saint Luc, said Jean-François. And even... and even...

Jean-François paused a moment, because he was about to say that his safe conduct was spurious and admirably imitated. He finished:

— And I'm even dying of hunger.

---

1. This story belongs to the time when France was cut in two by a kind of inner border and when, to go from one zone to another, it was necessary to have the safe-conduct of the Germans.

— We'll have lunch, right away, said Luc.

He called his old housekeeper and asked her:

— What do we have that's good today?

— Only rutabagas, like yesterday, Monsieur Luc, said the housekeeper.

— Ah! ah! and what else?

— Some non-rationed cheese, said the housekeeper.[2]

— Ah! ah! said Luc.

He looked at Jean-François with a guilty expression.

— There's still a bit of butter which Madame had sent from the country last week, said the housekeeper. But we don't have any bread to put it on.

— I have many bread tickets, exclaimed Jean-François. And even...

He caught himself again. These tickets had been stolen on behalf of the organization, by a town employee, and Jean-François had been on the verge of saying so.

— And I can even let you have them, added Jean-François.

The housekeeper grabbed the ticket-book with a kind of avid hardness and ran to a bakery.

— You're not doing very well by yourself, said Jean-François, raising his voice to his brother. You were a gourmand once.

— I still am, sighed Luc, but what do you want...

— And the black market, to get by that way? asked Jean-François.

---

2. That is to say, without any nutritional value.

— Old Marion is afraid of the gendarmes, said Luc. And me...

— And you too, Saint Luc, said Jean-François with great friendliness and a touch of disdain.

They took their meal in the kitchen, which was the only room where there was a fire. Luc kept his coat and cap on.

— I'm storing up heat, he said.

— Eh, well, me, I was so hot I almost died twice this morning, cried Jean-François.

He stopped himself once again and explained.

— In those crowded trains & subways it's stifling.

At that moment Jean-François remembered the furniture dealer and regretted having refused his invitation. Then he felt ashamed. He preferred an andouillette to the company of his brother whom he had not seen for two years. But as Luc asked about the details of his journey, Jean-François realized that if he had so much wanted to be in the dealer's back room, it was because there he could talk about his false *ausweis*, and have him admire the skill of the doctoring, and he could reveal the origin of his bread tickets, & above all he could have told him at length of his two long day's adventures and much more and laughed at the German and the French police. And the dealer whose shop served as a warehouse & relay point and mailbox, he would have known, for his part, a hundred great stories.

And Jean-François felt that the little junk shop dealer whom he had barely known was closer to him than the brother whom he had always cherished and whom he continued to cherish, but with whom he had nothing in common but memories. Life, real life, in all its warmth, in all its deep and powerful richness, he could only share it with people like Félix or the Bison, or the tubercular worker who had hidden him for two days, or like the locomotive engineer who helped him to smuggle weapons through and whose eyes were so clear even in their sheath of soot.

Jean-François had already experienced this feeling during the war, for his *Corps Franc* comrades. But then he could talk about them and about his existence among them to the whole of France. Now he had to hide everything, except from his companions of the secret war. And this made them, for Jean-François, his true people.

Félix had granted himself three days in Paris with Jean-François, but he took the train for the south that same evening.

Subsequently, he assured himself that he had had a premonition.

IV

While Jean-François was having lunch with his brother on Avenue de la Muette, Gerbier was receiving Félix in Lyon. Their meeting took place at a theater agency. The director had lent one of his offices to Gerbier, which enabled him to receive a procession of the strangest and most varied characters without attracting attention.

People who knew Gerbier and Félix best could not have detected the slightest change in their relations. But, since they had executed Dounat, they did not feel as natural as they once did when they were alone together. Therefore they spoke a little faster and in a somewhat more tense tone than previously.

— I sent for you because it's urgent, said Gerbier. They've searched the premises of our doctor friend, in the southwest sector. His entire infirmary was ransacked. Luckily, none of our people were hiding out there that day. He got away, but the place is done for.

— I see, I see, said Félix.

— How many people do you have in all to set sail for Gibraltar? Gerbier asked.

— Eh, well, the two Canadian Commando officers from Dieppe, you know them, and then three new fellas from the R.A.F. who fell by parachute, and two Belgians, in addition, were sentenced to death by the krauts.

— And one of our radiomen will go to a training course in England, and also a young girl, said Gerbier. That makes nine. Where do they wait for the submarine?

— Damn! said Félix, the doctor's house was so convenient. Another ratting S.O.L.[3] or one of Doriot's henchman. I'll ...

Félix clenched his fists, but didn't finish. He and Gerbier exchanged glances. And they had remembered Dounat.

— This is not the moment for that question, Gerbier said quickly. Where will we put them?

---

3. *Service d'Ordre Légionnaire*: a fascist paramilitary organization serving as a volunteer political police force. (TN)

— Can't we leave them in the woods in little groups? asked Félix.

— No, said Gerbier. They're already doing foolish things. The Canadian colonel goes to the café. He believes that he speaks French without an accent, and everyone knows what's what. The population of the village can be counted on, including the gendarmes. But he's just a talker.

— Or a drunk, said Félix.

— And then the submarine is returning from operations, continued Gerbier. They'll signal its passing to us only the day before it leaves. They must all be together somewhere close by.

Félix slowly rubbed his bald spot until it grew red.

— I'm looking around, but, apart from the doctor, we've no one on this coast, said Félix.

— Then, you scout the region and find some property, an inn, a factory that will receive our people, said Gerbier. Before forty-eight hours!

— It's chancy, said Félix.

— I very well know, said Gerbier.

He thought of the telegrams that he occasionally received from London in which the general staff expressed to him their astonishment at the organization's delays and indiscretions. And he added with a certain bitterness:

— We're not an insurance company free of all risk.

— With the conditions in which we work, it's rather the opposite, said Félix.

— Everything depends on the man you choose for this mission, resumed Gerbier. No need of an organizer or a great intelligence. It takes resolve, and especially a good, quick eye that can recognize standup people. It's a matter of instinct.

— I see, I see, said Félix … Well, then I've a guy made to measure. My friend from the *Corps Franc*. You've never seen him, but you know whom I'm talking about. He's got the flair of a bloodhound. Only he's in Paris. He had to deliver a new transmitter to Dubois this morning.

— And when will he return? asked Gerbier.

— In three days, Félix said.

— Why?

— He has a brother whom he hasn't seen since the war … I didn't know we'd need him so soon, said Félix.

— Oh! this family stuff … said Gerbier between his teeth.

— It's for me, this remark? asked Félix.

His voice was subdued, but so aggressive that Gerbier refrained from answering. Félix's eyes burned from insomnia, the edges of his eyelids were red, and his round face had an earthen color.

"He doesn't sleep enough, his nerves are shot," thought Gerbier. "But none of us sleeps enough."

Félix, seeing that Gerbier was silent, broke out again with the same inner violence:

— If the charge about the family is for me, it's a bit strong.

For a moment Gerbier didn't know what he was getting at. Then he remembered & asked:

— How's the little boy?

— Not well, said Félix. The doctor found nodes in his lungs …

— He must be sent to the country, said Gerbier.

— With what? asked Félix. You can well imagine that being all the time on the road, as busy as I am, on the spot with a thousand things, I don't have a minute to earn a *sous*. We just manage to eat, & that only because my wife works as a housekeeper. And she has her pride, my wife. Then she calls me useless, a loafer. And what can I tell her? And the kid left all alone in the humid workshop.

— You've never spoken to me of this, said Gerbier. We have the funds.

— Oh! I'm grateful, Monsieur Gerbier, said Félix ... Is it that I have a beggar's mouth, by chance?

With his nail, Gerbier absentmindedly scratched the wood of the desk behind which he sat. At that moment, Félix, the mechanic, reminded him of Roger Legrain, the young electrician with tuberculosis from Camp L. The same dignity ... The same sense of honor ... Gerbier's silence, now, greatly annoyed Félix.

— I didn't tell you all of that to complain, Félix murmured. I don't know what came over me ... When you spoke about family just now, I thought you, eh, well, that you were alone, that you weren't tied to anyone. That's lucky with the kind of work that we do.

Gerbier continued to scratch the table with his fingernail. He wasn't tied to anyone ... that was true. He had almost attached himself to Legrain. But Legrain had refused to escape ... That was lucky ...

— Then what do we do for this reconnaissance mission? Gerbier asked sharply.

— I'll go myself, said Félix.

Gerbier considered Félix's inflamed eyelids, the unhealthy color of his cheeks.

— You need a good night's rest, said Gerbier.

— That's not the issue, said Félix. But I swore to my wife & kid that I'd drive them to the cinema, next Sunday.

Félix could however keep that promise. He ran into Jean-François on the Paris-Nice express.

V

The farm was located midway between the big national highway and the sea. The spacious outbuildings, solidly built in the old style, formed a kind of horseshoe around the main house near the shore. Toward the horizon, close to the seashore, stretched cultivated fields, vineyards, and clusters of trees. Low walls enclosed those grounds. Jean-François, sitting by a trail with his bicycle lying beside him, was eyeing the farm. Of all the possible shelters that he had taken note of throughout the day, this one certainly seemed the most suitable. Jean-François jumped on the seat.

Chickens were pecking the dirt in the courtyard and an old farmhand was chopping wood on the porch steps.

— Where's the boss? Jean-François asked him.

The old man sat up with difficulty, and in a series of movements, wiped the back of his neck, patted his expressionless and sweaty face with his hand, and formed a sort of flag around his ear.

— I can't hear you, he said.

— The boss, Jean-François shouted.

The door opened and a woman in a black dress and shawl appeared. She was middle-aged, small, and held her head very straight.

— The boss isn't here; the boss is in town, she said, with the bright accent of the region.

Jean-François smiled at this subdued, common, and severe face.

— Never mind, Madame, he said. The real boss, I'm sure, is you.

Jean-François was wearing a heavy turtleneck sweater, old pants, bicyclist's socks, and old sport shoes. He had no hairstyle, his matted blond hair falling over his forehead. But because of his hands, his bearing, and his voice, the farmer's wife was sure that he belonged to the upper class.

— If it's for the black market, it's not worth it, she said. We've nothing to sell.

— Would you give me a drink, said Jean-François. My throat's on fire.

The young man's lashes & temple were coated in dust. The winter was very mild in the region. The roads were very dry.

— Come in, said the woman.

In the spacious living room, there was a fire in the tall chimney. The setting sun was making the polished wood of the old rustic furniture glimmer. From outside came the cracking sound of wood being split and the clucking of chickens. The farmer's wife put a bottle and a glass on the table.

— Water would have sufficed, said Jean-François.

— We never refuse wine to a traveler at Augustine Viellat's, even in times of distress, the woman said proudly.

Jean-François drank slowly. The pleasure that each sip gave him was visible on his clear face.

— Another glass? asked Augustine.

— Gladly, said Jean-François. It's good.

— It's from our land, said the farmer.

She watched Jean-François drink and restrained a sigh. She had no son, & she would like to have had a big boy like that: strong, beautiful, simple.

— You fought in the war? she asked.

— From beginning to end, said Jean-François, in the *Corps Francs*.

— The *Corps Francs*, replied Augustine, they were good soldiers.

— It's said, repeated Jean-François, laughing.

He suddenly got up, went over to the radio sitting on a trunk, switched it on, & flipped the dial to find the London station.

— It's not the time, said the farmer's wife.

She was standing near the table. Jean-François came and sat down next to the woman at the corner of the table.

— I must find a place to hide a few comrades before night-fall, he said.

No change came over the woman's face but she lowered her voice to ask:

— Are they escaped prisoners?

— They're British, said Jean-François.

— What do you mean British? exclaimed Augustine.

The surprise had caused her to raise her voice. And she glanced through the window with instinctive anxiety. She saw only the old deaf farmhand.

— Some are from the Dieppe affair and some are downed airmen, said Jean-François.

— Mother Mary... murmured Augustine. Mother Mary... British soldiers down here ... I thought we only found them in the Northern countries.

— That's where they began hiding, said Jean-François. They were treated wonderfully.

— I hope, said the farmer's wife. British soldiers are welcome in all good French homes.

Augustine had drawn her black shawl across her chest & trembled slightly.

— So, if I bring them to you? asked Jean-François.

— I will say thank you, said the farmer's wife.

— It's not without danger, I warn you, said Jean-François. With them there's also ...

— I think you're rather a bit young, my little one, to be giving me advice in my own house, interrupted Augustine.

— And what about their safety? asked Jean-François.

— My husband and daughter think the way I do, and the farmhand has been here since my stepfather's time, said Augustine impatiently.

— There are eight or nine of us, said Jean-François.

— The house is big.

— And for food? asked Jean-François.

— No one has ever died of hunger, thanks to God, even in these evil times, at Augustine Viellat's, said the farmer's wife.

VI

They arrived in small groups in two nights. The Canadian Commandos of Dieppe had gone through ten retreats: fisherman's cabins, squire's castles, mountain hamlets, roadside inns. The two wounded R.A.F. pilots had been tended to in a country doctor's home for weeks. The Belgian *francs-tireurs* had worked in a lumberyard as loggers. Finally, Félix brought a taciturn Pole who had had all the fingers of his right hand broken by the Germans before he had escaped.

To house those men in the attic, Augustine had stripped all the beds of their mattresses and taken out the finest linens from her armoires. To feed them she found raw hams smoked with herbs, preserved geese, eggs from the yard, salted butter, honey from the hills, and jams made on the farm with pure sugar. Her guests never knew that she was therefore sacrificing all the reserves accumulated for a winter of famine and that she was giving up all of her family's bread rations to them. This proud and despotic boss' wife cared for them with a solicitude full of timidity. The British & Canadians especially were the object of her veneration. They seemed to her to be somewhat remarkable beings. They came from so far away. They were still fighting.

— Be quiet then, Augustine told them when they thanked her for her attention. What would we have become without you?

And they who had received the same welcome throughout the whole of France, they smiled uneasily.

Jules Viellat who, due to his clubfoot, had been rejected in 1914 and in 1939, kept repeating to himself: "And me also, I make some war now." He said this sometimes, but only to his daughter Madeleine. To his wife, he didn't dare. Madeleine, who had black eyes & a Spanish complexion like Augustine, didn't know if she was more in love with the tall, broad, and affable Canadian colonel, or with the young pilot who had the face of a child. The Belgians made her laugh with their accents and racy little stories. The old farmhand, because he was born in a border village, believed that his bosses harbored smugglers. They let him believe it.

When night came, everyone gathered to listen to the English broadcasts in the large living room of the farmhouse where everything — doors & shutters — was carefully closed. Augustine contemplated those strange and foreign faces against the background of the old walls, amid the old furniture that had known only the same family of modest farmers, and shook her proud little head in disbelief. And when she thought that those men would soon leave in a submarine (the residents of the farm had said so — they felt that secure) it seemed to Augustine that she was already telling this story to the children Madeleine would have and that the little ones were listening as if to a fable.

That lasted about a week. Then, one evening, Jean-François returned. He announced that the departure would take place the following night. Augustine drew her shawl tighter across her chest to hide her agitated hands. As they were about to leave one another to go to sleep, Augustine detained Jean-François:

— I'd love to have others, if ever needed, she said to him almost timidly.

Her request didn't astonish Jean-François. Each time people began by happenstance to help the resistance, they were happy and wanted to continue.

Was it hatred against the enemy, a feeling of solidarity, or a taste for adventure that thus found satisfaction? Jean-François was not one to concern himself over the answer. But he knew that through this training the entire country was peopled with precious relays and innumerable complicities.

— There's no lack of customers, said Jean-François smiling to Augustine.

His blue eyes alighted for a moment on the wireless device that Jules Viellat was listening to.

— And then, said Jean-François, we might broadcast from your house.

— I don't understand, said the farmer's wife.

— We could talk to London, said Jean-François.

— Holy Virgin! exclaimed the farmer's wife. Talk to London! From our house! From my house! You hear, Jules! You hear, Madeleine?

— Careful, said Jean-François, you could suffer the death penalty.

Jean-François could hear the breaths of the Viellat family in the big room with its smoky rafters.

— What do you think, Jules? his wife asked.

— I want what you want, said Jules.

Augustine listened to the muffled trampling that was being made in the attic by the Canadians, Belgians, British, & the Pole as they were lying down and said:

— Then, I want it.

— I'll talk to my boss tomorrow, said Jean-François.

Gerbier arrived before daylight. With him he had an old & bearded radio operator & an insignificant-looking young woman.

Jean-François took Gerbier aside and told him:

— The fisherman awaits us tonight from ten on. He has a big boat. It can take everyone. This will save us multiple trips. The daughter of the house will take you to the spot across the fields to avoid the patrols.

— It's well conceived, said Gerbier.

— I return? asked Jean-François.

— No, said Gerbier.

He lit a cigarette and carried on:

— I have a mission for you. An important mission, my kid (his voice was particularly gentle and penetrating). You will take the big boss to the submarine. You hear, the big boss. He leaves too. And I don't want him to go aboard with the whole gang. It's risky. There are too many of us. You will leave with him — from another point — in a skiff. The Bison will bring him to you. Wait for my signal when I'm on board. Three blue dots and a dash.

— Understood. I'll answer for everything, said Jean-François.

He was delighted. He loved to row.

Augustine went down to serve breakfast to the new visitors.

— Since we're pressed for time this evening, Madame, I would like to know right away what I owe you, Gerbier said to her.

— Oh! murmured Augustine … Oh! how can you …

— But really … eight people for a week … in these difficult times, insisted Gerbier.

— And you, are we paying you by the day for what you do? Augustine asked sternly. No! Then I will have you know that, though we are peasants, the Viellats are as proud as you.

Gerbier thought of Legrain, of Félix, and went to breakfast in the kitchen. When he had finished, he said to Augustine, who had not deigned to look at him:

— I would like you to allow me to bring you something from London when I return.

— You … you will return, stammered Augustine, whose head was reeling a bit. Do they do that, too?

— Sometimes, said Gerbier.

— But it's much worse to begin again after having been in free countries.

— I don't know … It's my first trip, said Gerbier. And I would love to bring you back a souvenir.

Augustine quickly regained her breath and whispered:

— Weapons, give me weapons. They will serve the whole township, should the day come.

VII

The darkness was intense. Yet the ridges of the steep rocks that serrated the cove could be perceived in the depths of the night sky. A grotto formed at the bottom of the narrow and wild cut, which was shaped like a jagged arrow and through which the sea penetrated into the coast with a thousand detours.

Jean-François was lying on the sand at the bottom of the cove and so close to the water that the longest waves wet his bare feet. He wore linen trousers rolled up to his knees, an old wool sweater, and felt wonderfully comfortable in his light and loose clothes. Periodically, he shut his eyes to better hear what was going on in the hollow of the night, and the better to see thereafter. Jean-François had learned this in the *Corps Francs* during his watches, and he had learned to outsmart the night mirages that make enemies and fear out of nothing.

A gust scourged the sand. Jean-François was glad to feel it subside. He was not afraid of a swell. Of all the exercises at which he excelled, watersports were those that he did best. He knew his strength. He knew his prowess. Even in bad weather he was confident about taking the skiff that lay within reach of his hand to the British warship. But Jean-François preferred calm water for his passenger. He hadn't perhaps his sea legs.

Jean-François shut his eyes and was nothing more than a sort of listening antenna. Nothing stirred around him but the waves. Very far up, on the road that wound along the serrated coast, a feeble engine roared. It might be the Bison's car. Jean-François raised his eyelids. It was strange to think that the boss would soon take up in the boat and that he had the dimensions and weight of the whole world. Félix's team, if not Félix himself, had never approached him. He was nameless, formless, and yet on his orders we were going to prison, to torture, to death. He made arms drop from heaven, and ammunition surge from the waves. His existence was shrouded in a kind of sacred cloud. His departure had all the workings of a magic act. He came from no one knew where, and he was about to disappear into the sea.

And now Jean-François, who never thought to get serious, would serve as a ferryman to the big boss, the one who planned, organized, and commanded everything. Jean-François felt no pride, but a kind of gaiety. "The summit and the base of the pyramid meet," thought Jean-François. "Curious mathematics. I'll have to talk to Saint Luc about it after the war." Jean-François felt himself smiling in the night. Poor Saint Luc with his wool cap, his rutabagas, his fear of the gendarmes, all while life was so beautiful, so vast, so…

Jean-François raised himself lightly on his elbows. All thought was suspended in him. He was positive he heard someone stir at the edge of the rocks which, on the right side, sheltered the cove. The man must be very accustomed to the terrain. He made no more noise than lapping water carrying a stone. Now the silence was whole again. The boss was going to arrive from one moment to the next. And from one moment to the next the signal might flash in the night. That unknown scout should not see them. Jean-François began to crawl along the beach ... He was holding a rubber truncheon. Blending into the wet sand, light and slippery like a viper, Jean-François quickly crossed the edges of the cove. He then sensed, between two blocks of stone, another block, also still, but of a slightly greyer shade. It was a man.

Jean-François tightly gripped the handle of his truncheon in the hollow of his palm. The blow on the scout's head would not be fatal, but it would surely knock him out until dawn.

Jean-François advanced a few centimeters. He was now within range and gathered his strength. But the man suddenly disappeared behind a rock and Jean-Francis heard a muffled voice.

— No foolishness. I'm armed.

Two short waves broke one after the other against the point. Then the voice asked (& Jean-François felt it had the habit of authority):

— What are you doing here at this hour?

— And you? retorted Jean-François, ready to jump over the rock.

— I am Augustine Viellat's brother-in-law, said the invisible interlocutor.

— Jean-François let his body relax & murmured:

— Our farmer?

The man came out of his hiding place.

— I'm making a round to see if everything is going well with the departure.

— And so? asked Jean-François.

— Okay, okay, said the man. The gendarmes patrol passed up above. The krauts aren't yet numerous enough and they don't know the country. They trust customs.

— And customs? asked Jean-François.

— What customs? said the man. Good one! Customs … it's me. I'm the warrant officer for the entire sector.

— It's damn good, said Jean-François.

He put the truncheon back into his pocket.

VII

Sparks of bluish fire rose above the water, flickered and disappeared. Jean-François saw the signal & was on his feet at the same time. Almost immediately, on the path that led from the road to the bottom of the cove, he heard heavy and awkward footsteps. The silence was such that the noise of each step seemed to Jean-François to resound through the whole of France. He squeezed the handle of his truncheon and undid the safety catch of the revolver he had in his pocket. His orders were to ensure the departure no matter the cost.

After a few moments two shadows appeared & began to glide on the sand.

— Set off, murmured one of them.

Jean-François recognized the Bison's voice.

He put the skiff into the sea as close as he could to the shore & used all his strength to steady it.

Despite this, the passenger boarded so awkwardly that he almost managed to capsize the skiff.

"This one here hasn't been trained by the *Corps Francs*," thought Jean-François with impatience. He caught the skiff & found himself at the oars.

— Good luck, boss, whispered the Bison.

Only then, Jean-François remembered who the awkward passenger was. And the inexperience that he had shown before the elements seemed infinitely touching & respectable.

"If he was like me, he wouldn't be the big boss," said Jean-François to himself.

He no longer thought of anything but rowing the skiff as quickly and as silently as possible. The passenger was sitting in the stern.

The signal flashed once again. The distance to be covered to those fires was considerable. But Jean-François' arms rocked back & forth like oiled pistons. Finally, a vague form loomed low over the horizon, quite close. Jean-François gave a soft row of the oar. The skiff drew up against the hull of a barely emerged submarine.

Someone on board leaned forward. The luminous beam of a strong flashlight briefly illuminated the whole skiff. For the first time the two men who occupied it saw their faces torn from the night. The one who was rising with difficulty from the stern said in a muffled voice:

— My God … little Jean … is it possible?

And Jean-François recognized his elder brother.

— The boss, he stammered. Listen … how …

The flashlight flicked off. The night became blacker than before. Impenetrable. Jean-François took a blind step. As he touched his brother, he was lifted up by invisible arms. The submarine moved off, plunged down.

Reflexively, Jean-François launched the skiff into the wake that carried his brother away. Suddenly, drained of strength, he abandoned the oars. The skiff slowly drifted ... Jean-François had no idea how long it took him to understand and believe what had happened. Then he murmured:

— Holy Saint Luc ... What a family ...

Then he began to laugh & while singing, made his way to the shore on the dark sea.

4

THESE PEOPLE ARE WONDERFUL

They dined with candles that were tall, slender, and the color of rose tea. When the old lady received guests, she did not tolerate any other lighting. To her friends, she still looked a bit like the portraits of her that were spread throughout her salons and which had been painted during the reign of King Edward VII. The house overlooked Belgrave Square. The bombings had ruined many of the houses in the vicinity, but the old lady had consistently refused to leave hers. The servants being of an age that exempted them from military duties, she had been able to keep up her home and habits. One of them, formed in the time of the *Entente Cordiale*, was the holding of frequent gatherings of eminent Frenchmen in London. They could, without warning, and at the last minute, bring new guests. The man beside me was one such guest.

He had just come from France. He knew no one at the table, except the friend who had introduced him and who was seated far from him. The conversation was brilliant and substantive but hinged on facts and persons of whom he knew nothing. He heard the words and not the language. He was visibly bewildered, like a traveler who lands on an unreal shore and no longer recognizes the laws and customs of life.

This was not surprising to me. I was in the same situation as him. Our condition and our common solitude naturally attracted me to him. Aside from curly greying hair and a high, solid forehead, a simplicity *&* singular sweetness in the lines of his features made his face very appealing. He had very clear eyes, a bit tired, which rested alternately on the flowers, wall decorations, old servants, and the candelabra with an attentiveness simultaneously studious and enchanted. One felt in him the constant presence of an intense inner focus, but also a penchant for the fanciful *&* for deep candor. His character and his occupations had probably kept him free of the ordinary concerns of life. A professor ... a laboratory scientist ... perhaps a botanist.

— Everything around us is surprising, is it not? I asked him.

— More than surprising, he said with warmth. We have fallen on a plain miracle.

He had a somewhat weak voice but its power of persuasion was great.

— Life becomes so easy all of a sudden, he went on.

These words awakened an unease the weight of which I often felt in London.

— Too easy, I said.

He looked at me with sympathy (I realized later that he could not look at people otherwise) *&* I had the feeling that the freshness of his trade with life had its source not so much in naiveté but kindness.

— You think of the conditions in which we live at home, he said, and here you are embarrassed by the excess of white bread … and the hot bath every morning with soap that foams on the body.

He closed his thoughtful and clear eyes halfway.

— I am undoubtedly immoral, he said, but, honestly, I cannot bring myself to feel remorse. I accept things as they come.

The man beside me was one of those rare men whose presence incites one to think aloud. I remarked:

— You can't have left your ivory tower so often?

— Is that to say that I'm a bookworm, he said, laughing.

I shall never forget his laugh. It was barely audible, but its sound was so tender, so pure, and so assured, it cast a childhood luminosity upon the face of a man whom I admired and envied for being able to laugh in such a way at his age. He seemed to suddenly realize that the universe was offering him amusement and he was laughing just to hear himself laugh. It had an extraordinary charm.

— What made you guess so? The shape of my shoulders? My hair? he asked.

He tugged awkwardly at the bushy white tufts that curled over his temple and said:

— It's too long, I know. But I cannot bring myself to go to an English barber. I'm so used to ours. They are wonderful people.

An exaltation so sudden on his part, and connected to such a subject, struck me as a bit absurd. I must have betrayed my feelings because he began to laugh again. And as he had not stopped fingering his greying hair, his very youthful laugh was still more seductive.

— I wasn't thinking of the touch of the hand, he said, no, not really…

He shook his head & continued:

— In Paris, I regularly visit a barbershop on the Left Bank. It's a modest place. The owner works there himself with two employees. His wife tends the till. They have a little boy and a little girl who, after school, do their homework in the back room. A family outside of history. Yet one morning, as I entered my barber's, he suddenly left the customer who he was accommodating, dashed to another waiting his turn, snatched a short printed sheet from his bare hands, and shouts at me: "Look, look what just arrived, Monsieur. This is what I found in my mail." He was holding a copy of a clandestine newspaper. "The articles in it are great, the boss said. Against the krauts, against the collaborators, with names, details, everything. It takes courage to print such things. Isn't that true, gentlemen?"

And everyone, with their lathered faces, those who were under scissors or clippers, everyone agreed. The clandestine newspaper had gone round the shop. "Imagine, they sent it to me. To me!" said the guy. He beamed with pride. "It's really a great honor that they're doing us," his wife at the counter said softly. "Read quickly," whispered the boss. "I'm expecting a lot of people this morning, everyone must get a chance to read it." For a *sous*, he would have posted the thing in his window.

— That was before or after the circulation of resistance papers was punishable by death? I asked.

— After, long after, said my acquaintance.

He laughed. His face expressed the most astonished, the most tender admiration. One would have said that this story was all new to him. One would have thought that I had just made it known to him.

— Barbers are wonderful people, he assured.

Meanwhile the dinner was ending. The butler served *crème au chocolat*. It was rich and light, as smooth to the tongue as to the eye. One had to come from France to appreciate this incredible thing to the full.

— Ah ... said my acquaintance.

He ceased talking to abandon himself in all innocence to his delectation. Then he murmured:

— This dinner is an enchantment.

His serious and chimerical gaze slowly passed along the table at the end of which we were sitting. And, following that gaze, I became conscious again of the beauty of the flowers, the cutlery, the crystal, & the charm of the lights. This man's story had made me forget all that. But he seemed to possess the gift of enjoying unadulterated pleasure from the blessings of a happy home, and, simultaneously, of keeping in his mind the torments and the secret efforts of a people at the mercy of a cohort of spies, jailers, and executioners.

— A true enchantment, said my acquaintance. We owe much to this old lady, who doesn't even know us.

The hostess sat very straight in the middle of the table. Her small and delicate head emerged from a black organdy collar. That color and that material gave more luster to the brilliant whiteness of her hair. Her eyes were still exceptionally vivacious. We were sitting too far away to hear well what she was saying, but the inflections of her lips were full of intelligence, will, and wit.

— Women are wonderful beings, said my acquaintance.

And as I had, once again, misunderstood the meaning of his ardor, he added in a half-joking, half-guilty tone:

— You know, it's quite separate from any *crème au chocolat* … I remember a woman named Mathilde who had a bailiff clerk for a husband. I didn't know her, but I often heard about her from a student of mine.

("He is surely a professor," I thought.)

"This student's favorite pastime, when she was traveling by metro, was to put contra-German tracts in the pockets of German officers & soldiers. She lived on the same floor as Mathilde in a moderately-priced barracks building, built by the City of Paris for the petit bourgeoisie. But while the student led a carefree existence in her bachelor's quarters, with perfect sexual freedom, the bailiff clerk, his wife, and their seven children, they suffocated in a three-room apartment. Mathilde was jaundiced, gaunt, exhausted by her domestic obligations, and perhaps because of this, of very aggressive virtues. Moreover, my friend was anarchistic and Mathilde, just as her husband, was fanatical about *Action Française*. In short, they hated each other as only two women can.

"One day, and solely as a jest, the student slipped a leaflet into Mathilde's coat. But the bailiff's wife had a more vigilant eye than an occupation soldier. You see, she spent her life watching over her children, watching her gas, and seeing to it that she wasn't being robbed. She seized the student's wrist and read the leaflet.

"Finally, I've got my hands on one of them, thank you, my God!" said Mathilde.

The scene was happening on the stairway of the house. "Let's go to your place," Mathilde ordered. My friend was desperate to avoid a public incident. She obeyed.

"In the bachelor pad the bed was unmade. Makeup, very personal grooming items, and empty bottles were scattered around. Mathilde recoiled. She murmured: "I never would have thought …" But the disgust that spread across her long face suddenly gave way to an expression of appeal. She clasped the hands of the young girl in her two strong hands & said, "Mademoiselle, you have to help me." "Help you?" repeated the student blankly. "Against the krauts," said Mathilde. And suddenly this utterly taciturn and rigid woman, this woman who seemed as sterile in her feelings as in her features and her body, this woman was seized by an attack of passion. She spoke of the hunger of her children, of futile lines, torturous winters without coal, of her husband's pulmonary congestion, hunting for clothes, and going without shoes. None of her words had the tone of a complaint. They expressed a fierce revolt against the Germans. The only despair for Mathilde was to remain inactive. But what to do? She knew no one in the resistance circles. Her husband (a poor man, she had realized) still believed in the Marshal. "I want to work toward the defeat of the krauts, Mathilde finished. Nothing will be too difficult, painful, or dangerous for me. I want to help destroy the krauts." Not once during this crisis had Mathilde raised her voice. But the violence of her remarks, the quivering of her thin lips and waxen cheeks, the almost unbearable sparkle of an ordinarily prudent and lifeless gaze, revealed more about my friend than screaming would have done. "You will work in my circuit distributing our leaflets, she said. You know nothing else and you will take orders only from me." I think that upon hearing the name of the newspaper and gazing once at the indecent disorder of the room, Mathilde must have waged an obscure struggle against her conscience. But she accepted. First she was entrusted part of a street, then the whole street, then a whole district. It was an immense task that she accomplished methodically & with flawless attention to detail. She didn't argue. She always had time for everything. She was never weary. She would go to the food lines earlier. She mended the clothes & did the laundry later. It was nobody's business. Her husband knew nothing.

"Sometimes, when she came early to her next-door neighbor's to receive instructions, she would find a strange man in the student's bed. "A fighting comrade," the latter would say. Mathilde smiled an expressionless smile, listened to the orders, then left. She had grown still thinner but her face no longer expressed hostility against life. She was especially happy when it was necessary to add explosives to the thick bundles of leaflets. And do you know how she went about getting them through Paris? She put the papers, and occasionally the sticks of dynamite, in the bottom of her little carriage, which served for her newborn, a baby of eighteen months. Two of her older little girls would accompany her — their cloaks were stuffed with copies of underground literature. Who could have suspected this gaunt, serious-looking woman taking her malnourished children out for air?"

Everyone left the dinner table and went into the large living room. So did we. But I had been quite unaware of it since my acquaintance was able to absorb me in the life of this parched silhouette of a woman with her faded, carefully mended clothes, who from morning till night would, through starving and tragic Paris, wheel a malnourished baby on a bed of forbidden newspapers & explosives.

— Mathilde, however, ended up being caught through an indiscretion that didn't come through her, said my acquaintance. Nothing could make her talk. When I left France, the police had not yet decided her fate.

Servants with white whiskers were passing coffee, alcohol, cigarettes, & cigars. And my acquaintance remarked:

— I don't smoke, but I like being around Virginia or Havana tobacco. Especially here. You feel how that odor is suitable for this place?

The man beside me had the ability of making me teeter constantly from one universe to another. But while his mind balanced out, easily giving in to dramatically and almost monstrously contrasting visions, I regarded this rich & warm room, this abundance, this safety, with a kind of metaphysical terror.

I was still so close to the French suffering and struggle, and so marked by its climate, that the famished, oppressed, threatened & subterranean life seemed most natural to man in these times. It is likely that in mingling with the group formed around our hostess, & helped by the faculty that is dormant in most people, I could forget, joking and smoking my cigar and drinking whiskey with peace of heart. This had already happened to me in London. If now kept from this, it was due to my companion. Yet I didn't think to leave him.

— In the Rue de Lille, there's a perfect French replica of the mistress of the house, he said. Her salons are a bit steely, the meals lean, and the cigarettes cut in four, as everywhere else. But as for the vitality, the cult of traditions, the spirit and the despotic temperament, my dowager countess is in no way inferior to this charming old lady.

— You're a regular at the Faubourg Saint-Germain? I couldn't help asking.

— The countess has a Steinway with an admirable tone, my acquaintance replied, laughing. I would sometimes play music at her house.

I regarded him with renewed attention. Why had I decided that he was a scientist? His curly hair, his strong forehead, serious & ingenuous eyes, & the quality of his laugh? But all these traits could as well, if not better still, apply to an artist.

Someone put a jazz record on the phonograph hidden away in a corner of the immense room.

— At least these tunes are so pleasant that they don't impede conversation, said my acquaintance. There used to be music — real music — in the Faubourg Saint-Germain, but there was also conspiracy. The old countess had put in play all the relationships at her disposal, all the influences, all the suitors she had had in a very long sentimental life and which was reputed to have been very full. There were many senior officials among those friends from another age. She terrorized them, made them repudiate the Marshal, forced them into commitments. The writing desk where her grandmothers hid notes written by Lauzun and by the Duke of Richelieu was overflowing with false identity papers, fake mission orders, blank safe-conduct passes, recommendation letters to judges, police commissaires, prison directors. The Countess is senselessly imprudent. But her somewhat comical despotism saves her. "She's an old madwoman," people say, and they let her be ...

Another record ... another jazz tune. The man beside me continued:

— The countess has a great-nephew around thirty, with a flat and concave chest, almost bald, pimply, and who with his thin fingers, thin as filaments, constantly scratches his pimples. Poor education, rejected, no profession, a meager income. The portrait of the no-account son of a socially prominent family. He went into the resistance because he had always run errands for his great aunt. A wonderful type.

This time I exclaimed:

— One begs to know why?

— Because, said the man beside me, because this boy had become the best of liaison agents. Despite his dismal health, he spent weeks on the train without sleeping and almost without eating. He forced his way through barricades, smelled out mousetraps. He came close to death nearly ten times, continuing to scratch his pimples with his spindly fingers. He was caught and roughed up a bit. They couldn't bleed a word out of him. The old countess managed to free him. When he returned home from prison, he could hardly drag himself about. His pimples had become wounds. It was the only time he spoke of his feelings. "I think no one can accuse me of having laid out during the war," he had said.

This clarity cast upon a whole life surprised me to the point that I was unable to restrain an exclamation. My acquaintance began to laugh.

— Isn't it an astonishing cure for an inferiority complex? he asked me.

I said:

— You really know a lot of people, & many of their secrets.

— I practice a trade that calls for confidences, said the man beside me.

His laughter had become even more silent than usual. I looked back at the man and I thought: "In reality might he not be a neurologist, a psychiatrist?"

But while I was questioning his face, he suddenly turned and became as it were inaccessible. Another record had been put on the phonograph: it was a Bach oratorio. It had a sovereign, calming power. I was finally comfortable in the Belgrave Square salon, amongst the sumptuous paneling and the trembling tips of the candles magically multiplying in the mirrors.

And I was able to open this room and its luxury and its tranquility to that little barber, to those students, to Mathilde, to that disgraced family son. And I loved them all the more for being among us: hunted, ill-clad, malnourished, numb and addled with the humble and sacred mystery of their courage.

The great movement of the organ had elapsed. Gradually the conversations resumed.

— The last time that I played that oratorio, Thomas was listening, said my acquaintance. I have never had a friend like him and I have never met a man of purer knowledge, or of loftier spirit.

The man beside me spoke in his habitual tone, that is to say, fluid and peaceful. I realized however that his friend had died a tragic end. He guessed that I had understood.

— Yes, he replied with gentleness, Thomas had been shot, with a bullet in the nape of the neck, in the cellars of Hotel Majestic. Yet he was in a province when the little group of scientists who together with him had been sending information to London were discovered and arrested. He could have hidden. But it seemed to him impossible not to share the fate of his companions. He returned to Paris, he claimed the greatest responsibility, & he was granted the wish to be executed last, after seeing his friends fall.

I quite naturally waited for the man beside me to add to this story the word "wonderful," which was as familiar to him as a tic. But the word did not come. Undoubtedly, for my acquaintance, with a certain degree of spiritual elevation, nothing was astonishing.

I kept silent and the man beside me laughed to himself. I don't know how to make this felt, but it was impossible to better honor a dead friend than by that laughter.

And my acquaintance went off, stooping a bit, pushing back his grey curls with his hand.

Philippe Gerbier, who is an old comrade, approached me.

— Do you know the name of the man who left the salon? I asked him.

— Saint Luc, if you like, said Gerbier with his half-smile.

— You know him well?

— Yes, said Gerbier.

He lit a new cigarette with the one that he was finishing smoking and added:

— He'll be in France in a few days, with the next moon.

I took off very quickly.

In the streets, soldiers were embracing girls in uniforms. Joyous voices were hailing taxis.

The next moon? The next moon, I thought, looking at the sky cut in pieces by the beams of a searchlight. The next moon …

I remembered the joy of this man whose real name or whose real job I did not know, before the *crème au chocolat*, before the smell of Virginia tobacco … And his face as he listened to Bach's oratorio.

Shall I see you again, one day, my neighbor with the eyes of a child and a sage, you who laughed free of care, my neighbor … wonderful?

5

PHILIPPE GERBIER'S NOTES

Returned yesterday from England. When diving from the plane into the dark night, I remembered J. He had made a bad jump and broken both his legs. He nevertheless buried his parachute and dragged himself for five to six kilometers to the nearest farm where he was taken in. For my part, acute heart strictures when the pilot signaled to me. Fear for no reason. No wind. Landed in a plowed field. Buried the parachute. Knowing the region, had no difficulty finding the little local railway station.

Farmers, artisans, railroad men waiting for the train. First the usual conversation: food, food, food. Few markets, requisitions becoming intolerable, no heating. But also a new one: the deportations. Not a family, they said, that was not affected or about to be. They were envisaging ways of protecting their sons, nephews, and cousins from this expulsion. Prison atmosphere. Prisoners revolting. Natural hatred. They had likewise discussed the war news. Those who had a radio gave the others details about the London broadcasts. I was reminded that I had spoken over the B.B.C. on behalf of the French engineers two days before.

Left the train at the small town of C. I didn't want to rejoin our H.Q. of the southern zone directly. The last telegrams sent to London were worrisome. Went to an architect friend of ours. He received me as one receives a ghost. "You come from England, you come from England," he kept repeating. He recognized my voice from the radio. I didn't know it was so characteristic. I've made a rather stupid and quite serious impudence. Indiscretions are due not so much to malevolence, the temptation to talk, or even foolishness, as to admiration. Our people are mostly over enthused. They like to aggrandize, to exalt our comrades, and especially the bosses. It keeps them going, inflames them, and gives poetry to their monotonous little daily tasks. "You know, X has done a magnificent thing," said one in the know to another. And he needs to share his enthusiasm with a third. And so on. And the story reaches the ears of an informer. There is nothing so dangerous as that generosity of feelings.

Yet, because I had been to London, I risked becoming an object of worship. I saw this in the way in which the architect treated me. He is a man of substantial character and spirit. Yet he looked at me as if there was something a bit miraculous about me. That I returned did not astonish him too much. But the fact that I had spent a few weeks in London, that I had breathed the air of London, that I fraternized with the people of London, bewildered him. He considered those holidays, those days of comfort and of safety, as an act of the rarest merit. To explain such an attitude, in appearance a bit absurd, is rather simple. When everything seemed lost,

England was the only source of hope and warmth. For millions of Europeans, it was the fire of faith in the night. And all those who have approached and approach again this fire take on a wonderful luster. Among the Muslims, the pilgrim who goes to Mecca bears the title of Hadj, and wears a green turban. I am a Hadj. I am entitled to the green turban of an enslaved Europe. That seems pretty ludicrous, because I have no feeling for religion. But also because, me, I came back from London. Over there, the point of view is exactly the opposite.

Over there, it's living in France that seems admirable. Hunger, cold, privations, the persecutions that we have become accustomed to by force, have deeply affected their imagination and sensitivity. As for the people of the resistance, they arouse an almost mystical emotion. One feels the legend already taking shape. If I said that here, they'd shrug their shoulders. No woman who grumbles for hours in lines, who weeps with impotence upon seeing her anemic children, curses the government & the enemy for taking her husband to send him to Germany, who grovels to the milkman and the butcher to get a drop of milk or a gram of meat, never would such a woman believe that she is an exceptional person. And the boy who, every week, carries an old suitcase full of our underground newspapers, the transmitter who taps out our radio messages, the young girl who types my reports, the doctor who heals our wounded, and especially Félix, and especially the Bison, never would any of those people believe that they are heroes, & I don't believe it either.

Subjective opinions and feelings have no value. The truth is only in facts. I want, when I am free, to keep a record of the facts that may affect a man whom events have put at a good observation point to the resistance. Much later, with hindsight, those accumulated details will in sum allow me to form a judgment.

If I survive.

———————

Spent the night at the architect's. Had a visit from our sector boss. A railroad man. Former secretary of the syndicate. Very red. Excellent organizer. Character beyond reproach. If all the groups of the nation were as united and as resolute as the railroad men, our groups wouldn't have much to do.

That man confirmed for me the bad impression I got from the telegrams. Searches, raids, snares. The Gestapo wants to decapitate the resistance. It strikes close ten times, but they end by striking home. Our C.P.s discovered in Lyon, Marseille, Toulouse, Savoy. Three transmitters seized. We still don't know what's happening in the northern sector, but in the south, it's serious. My assistant, a petty registry official, bilious & indefatigable, has been summarily executed. My secretary deported to Poland. Félix arrested.

Lemasque, apparently, has done very well. He has set up an emergency C.P. in his office. Gradually, as the others fell, that C.P. has taken on importance. Lemasque has replaced the missing comrades with new ones. He proved to be quick, energetic, effective. But I fear for his nerves. I return just in time.

The railroad men advise my not dwelling too long with the architect. Too known as a Gaullist. The town is small.

———————

My host now is the Baron de V. And my housing a beautiful Louis XIII castle. The estate includes a park, a forest, a pond, rich and extensive lands. One cannot imagine a safer and more pleasant refuge. I can restore the connections and form plans with tranquility. The baron puts himself entirely at my service. He is a character. A long nose, his skin burnt by sun and wind, small and hard eyes — there is something both of the wolf and the fox about him. He loves only his land and hunting. Former cavalry officer of course. His wife and children live in terror of him. The only person who can stand up to him is his older sister, a spinster who is never out of her riding pants. The Baron de V was a sworn enemy of the Republic. Before the war, with his farmers, whipper-ins, and huntsmen, he formed an armed platoon with shotguns and revolvers that, in the event of a royalist insurrection, was designed to eliminate the neighboring prefecture by cavalry charge. This platoon, perfectly organized, perfectly trained, still exists. But it will act against the Germans. Weapons are not wanting. We made many parachute drops on the baron's land. He belongs to no resistance organization. But he helps them all. Once his wife and children are in bed, he sets off with his sister, both on horseback, to receive the parachutists.

It's to this feudal lord that our sector boss, the secretary of the syndicate, entrusted me. I joked with the Baron de V about his alliance with a revolutionary. He said to me: "I prefer, Monsieur, a red France to a blushing France."

———

News of Félix through Jean-François.

Félix was arrested in the street by two men speaking perfect French but who were Gestapo agents. He was questioned without suffering too many blows. Since he did not admit his identity, three Gestapo men took him to his home, in the dead of night. His wife and his little boy, terrified as they were, yet knowing nothing of Félix's underground activities, were not afraid of recognizing him. The German agents struck Félix in front of his wife and son until he fainted. Then, they began a search, smashing everything in the room. Félix came to, and he made a move to get up. He was clobbered again. The search continued. Félix came to again. This time, he didn't move. He had the sang-froid to lie still and recover, as Jean-François put it, and suddenly he rushed to the window, broke through the shutters, and jumped into the street. His room was on the second floor. He dislocated his ankle, but he ran all the same. A patrol of French bicycle agents was passing. Félix told the sergeant the truth. They took him to one of our people. The next day, Félix was in one of our clinics. The day after that, in another, and the following day, in yet another. It was only there that the Gestapo had lost track of him. Félix has a light cast. He will be released soon. He asks me for a new assignment. He won't be able to see his wife and little boy again until the war is over. He thinks that his wife is angry with him.

———

A teacher from Lyon took advantage of his Sunday to spend two nights on the train and bring me the mail. He falls asleep just before catching the train. He is so malnourished that he often forgets the rudiments in the class that he teaches. As for the children, he no longer dares send them to the blackboard. Their legs don't carry them anymore. They faint from hunger.

———

A country priest came to say mass at the castle. He spends his days and nights running from farm to farm: "You," he said to a farmer, "you have room for hiding three men who refuse to go to Germany." "You," he said to another, "you have two to feed," and so on. He knows everyone's resources. He has a lot of influence. They obey him. He was reported to the Germans and warned by the French authorities. "I must hurry," he said. "Before going to prison, I would like to put three hundred in place." It is now a kind of sport. A race against time.

———

The number of deserters who refuse to work in Germany ran to a few thousand by the time I left. They now number in the tens of thousands. Many are absorbed by the countryside. But many also take refuge in natural hiding places and occupy the maquis. The maquis of Savoie. The maquis of Cévennes. The maquis of Massif Central. The maquis of the Pyrenees. Each accounts for an army of young people. They must be fed, protected, given as much ammunition as possible. This is a new and terrible problem for the resistance.

Some groups have organized themselves into communities. They publish papers occasionally. They have their laws. A kind of tiny republic. Others salute the colors daily. The Cross of Lorraine flag. The next mail for London includes photographs of those ceremonies.

But most of those guys — young workers, students, clerks, employees — need an allied and strong leadership, money, connections. Appointed a committee of three from our organization to look after them: Félix, Lemasque, & Jean-François. They have virtues and faults that are complementary.

———

Sent off a reception team for people and parcels from England. Team composition: a fireman, a butcher, a town clerk, a gendarme, a doctor. Means of transport: the gendarmerie car and the butcher's van.

———

Good day:

1. A transmitter is operating at the home of the farmer's wife who harbored us before our departure in the submarine.

2. Félix came out of the clinic with his ankle entirely healed and a well-formed beard. He made it known that he's in contact with Lemasque.

3. Arrival of Mathilde.

She escaped with sixty detainees from the Palais de Justice in Paris where they had been taken for questioning. She does not know how it was arranged or by whom. Internal complicities in all probability. On a given word, they only had to follow the corridors as far as the door giving on to Place Dauphine, open it and walk out.

Mathilde remained in hiding in Paris for three days. She resisted the fierce desire to see her children. She had never done and will never do anything so hard. She showed me a photograph that she managed to conceal from every search. Six children, from the eldest, a girl of seventeen years, to the baby Mathilde, whom she wheeled around for a long time on stacks of forbidden newspapers. "I'm sure my eldest Thérèse will take care of the little ones. Me, I won't be able to tend to them, not until the end of the war," said Mathilde. She took the photograph back and hid it again. She asked for work right away, a lot of work, and dangerous. I said I would think on it a little. I know she can do a lot and do it well. She must be used at her best. Meanwhile, she remains at the castle.

———

Examined many reports.

For the people of the resistance, the margin of life is constantly narrowing. The Gestapo arrests multiply & the death sentences of the German courts multiply. And now, the French police automatically book the Frenchmen they hold at the enemy's request. Before, there was the prison, the concentration camp, the forced residence, even a simple warning from the authorities. Today, it is almost always death, death, death.

But, on our side, we kill, kill, kill.

The French were not prepared, not disposed to kill. Their temperament, their climate, their country, the state of civilization they had reached, warded them off bloodshed. I remember how, in the early days of the resistance, it was difficult to envisage cold-blooded murder, ambushes, planned assassinations. And how it was difficult to recruit people for that. There is no question now of such repugnance! Primitive man has reappeared in the French. They kill to defend their home, their bread, their loves, their honor. They kill every day. They kill the German, the traitor, the informer. They kill for a reason and they kill by reflex. I will not say that the French people have hardened. They have grown sharper.

———

In coming from Paris, Mathilde traveled part of the way with the dowager countess at whose house the boss used to visit to listen to music. The countess had with her a young British submachine gunner, hidden until then. When changing trains, they had to spend two hours in a waiting room. Suddenly, an identification check. The Englishman had none. He didn't know a word of French. The old lady made him crouch on the floor and sat over him. She spread her old-style long skirts all around him. The police didn't see a thing. The general complicity of travelers, naturally.

Long talks with Mathilde. I knew through the boss that she was a remarkable woman, but she amazed me all the same. She is made to organize, to command, and at the same time to serve. She sees simply and clearly. She sees justly. She has a will, a method, patience, & an equally powerful hatred of the Germans. Now that all her family ties have been cut by the enemy she has become a formidable instrument against him.

In prison, Mathilde learned a lot about disguises, about forms of evasion, about attack techniques. I take her as a deputy. She will tour the entire southern sector and contact the heads of each zone. She will rejoin me in a big city. The liaisons here are much too slow.

Chance? Luck? Premonition? Instinct?

I left the castle one week ago. Two days later, the Baron de V had been taken at the same time as our railroad man and our sector boss. They have already been shot.

———————

France is a prison. One feels the threat, the misery, the anguish, the misfortune, like a heavy vault that is collapsing and which comes closer to our heads every day. France is a prison, but illegality is an extraordinary escape. Papers? They are fabricated. Ration tickets? They are stolen from town halls. Cars, gasoline? We take them from the Germans. Troublemakers? They are suppressed. The laws, rules, no longer exist. The outlaw is a shadow that slips through their networks. Nothing is difficult, since we started with the most difficult: neglecting what is essential — the instinct of conservation.

———————

A travel scene.

My train stops at the Toulouse station longer than it should. Gestapo agents examine our ID cards. They're in my car (third class). They're in my compartment. No incident. Their footsteps recede. But another policeman comes and beckons a passenger to follow him. The passenger turns his back on the German; he stoops as if to pick up a newspaper he has dropped. And we all see that he takes a revolver that is hanging under his arm, removes the safety catch, then puts it in his coat pocket. All this of course very naturally, very fast. A perfect calm. The passenger takes his suitcase and leaves. The train doesn't start. The passenger reappears.

"He made a mistake," he said, resuming his place. He cuts a cigarette in two and smokes half. Conversations resume in the compartment.

A travel scene.

In the corridor of the third class coach, where people are jammed together, a young girl occasionally casts a quick glance at a fairly large package wrapped with cheap paper, placed a few meters from her. Travelers trampling one another. Getting on and off at train stops, people crush one another. The package is torn; it bursts open. The girl walks away. The package contents scatter. There are piles of clandestine newspapers. The passengers pick them up. The young girl has disappeared.

Result of a lack of suitcases, paper, and strong twine.

As night fell a resistance group removed many manhole covers in Marseille. Of the Germans and the friends of the Germans, who were the only ones allowed out after curfew, there was no one to regret among those who suffered broken bones at the bottoms of the sewers.

At all the major railway stations, the Gestapo and the French police, who were obeying their orders, posted men gifted with exceptional visual memory & who had carefully studied the photographs of the patriots they are searching for. They are "physiognomists" similar to the spotters found in the door-ways of gambling rooms in big casinos, and whose role was to remember the face of every player.

———————

The Gestapo gladly uses elderly, debonair, decorated men for its shadowing. People are less suspicious of those greying gentlemen. When you're tracked down by one of them, the danger is not yet imminent. They track, locate, and provide information. But if you then see younger and stronger men appearing in their wake, you must be ready for anything.

———————

I live in a big city, at the house of a magistrate, as his ser-vant. It's a good cover. Unfortunately, I always have to receive a great many people. Such coming and going is noticed very quickly in a quiet house. I won't be able to stay here long.

———————

Mathilde returned from her tour. She has given me a com-plete report on our sectors. She saw everyone. She spent every night in trains. It's less tiring, she said, than dealing with a large family when one is poor. In truth, she no longer looks like a housewife.

I think that her new way of life and a cold, desperate fury transformed her expression & her way of moving. But she's also been working at it as well. She said that during her journey, she changed her personage several times. Sometimes, she powdered her hair and wore an austere black dress. Sometimes, she painted herself up and dressed gaudily. "I pass fairly easily from the old genteel patroness to the old strumpet," she said in her matter-of-fact way.

One of the most important things that she had done was to mediate with the local bosses of other groups, to avoid overlapping and interference in operations. Sometimes two or three different organizations simultaneously work on the same objective: sabotage, derailment, attack, or execution. When working with no contact, the number of men is multiplied by two or three, unnecessarily, as are the risks. And that makes for one or two squads that could be used elsewhere. It is equally important to avoid the risk of a minor operation bringing the police down on a place where a larger operation is being prepared. Obviously, the exchange of plans increases the chances of leaks & indiscretions.

It's the eternal problem of the secret life. You cannot recruit, you cannot act without trust and confidence, yet confidence is reckless. The only remedy: divide to limit the damage. The Communists are the masters of such divisions, as everything in the subterranean city. Mathilde returns marveling at the strength, discipline, & method that she encounters in their homes. But short of making underground action for a quarter century, we cannot match them. They are professionals; we're still paying our dues.

———————

Mathilde found an attic in the house of a little seamstress. She said that she was a nurse. She will have her papers tomorrow. She will direct one of our fighting units.

———————

I'm still with the judge. He is nothing more to the organization than a friend who is ready to help. But a standup friend. He has just investigated a Gaullist case in which four of our people were accused. One of the four, when arrested, made a confession that led to jailing three others. The judge was able to convince the informant to retract his statements and put them entirely down to police brutality (which was real). The judge said to him: "My findings will provide you with the most lenient penalty."

In truth, he did everything to ensure that the informer remained imprisoned as long as possible. We don't have prisons. This is a chance that can sometimes work to our benefit in regard to those from Vichy.

Every evening, the judge recounted to me the progress of the case. The three comrades will come to know how they were released only after the war …

If they survive, and if I survive.

The boss is in Paris.

I relay to him verbally, via Jean-François, a large stack of mail. Jean-François returned. The boss agrees that Félix, Lemasque, and Jean-François oversee the maquis at once. The boss approves the position I entrusted to Mathilde.

On his way to Paris, Jean-François was carrying a suitcase of tracts. He had also put a ham in the suitcase. He feels sorry for his brother. As a matter of fact, the boss is dying of hunger … In the street, Jean-François had been seized by a *garde mobile* and had to open his suitcase. The guard had examined the contents thoroughly. He had a very hard face. Jean-François was preparing to throw it to the ground and flee. But the guard only said: "You oughtn't to mix up the black market with the work against the krauts. It's not clean." When Jean-François told his brother the story, the boss was very moved by it. Far more than by the adventures where so many of our people lose their lives.

The Gestapo has huge sums for its informers. We know a small town of 10,000 inhabitants where the Gestapo budget is a million francs per month. With that, they had bought four well-placed bastards. We could liquidate them fairly easily. But I think it's better to keep them until the final settlement. The traitors whose faces are known are less dangerous.

———————

We have friends throughout the enemy camp. And I even wonder if the enemy suspects how numerous, active, and well distributed they are. I'm not even speaking of the Vichy authorities. There is not one sub-prefecture, town hall, gendarmerie, supply office, prison, police station, or minister's office where our people are not set up. Every time one of our comrades is at risk of being handed over to the Gestapo, Laval finds a note on his desk warning him that he will be held accountable for our comrade.

With Vichy, the thing is not difficult. But even among the Germans themselves, we have our plants.

———————

The Bison is still perfect. Mathilde asked him for four German uniforms. The Bison got them.

This certainly means the death of four German soldiers. We will never know how the Bison did it. He has the silence of a Legionnaire.

Mathilde astonishes and impresses him. He said of her: "She's someone."

———————

Moved. Apartment under a fifth alias. Papers: colonial officer on leave. Inoculation against malaria: Mathilde, as a nurse, comes to administer the shots.

———

L, who is in General de Gaulle's services, arrives from London. This is his fifth trip. He had a lot of work before his departure. Two sleepless nights. Flying. Parachute. Twelve kilometers on foot. The train in the early morning. Falls asleep. His head falling hard against his neighbor, he wakes up. He believes he is still in England. He says, "Oh! I am so sorry."[4] He rubs his eyes — his neighbor was a German officer. No unfortunate consequences.

———

For his last departure for London, L took his family with him. He needed to protect them. The family included his wife, two young girls (aged 6 and 4), and a baby of 18 months. This is L's story:

"I had arranged it with a fisherman who was anxious to get to England. He had rigged his boat. In the morning, before going on board, I woke my daughters. It was still dark. I told them to be silent and to pray with more attention and faith than usual. Then I told them that we were going on a

———

4. In English in the original. (TN)

very dangerous sea voyage and that we might not see each other again if God was not with us. The boat was anchored in a small river. We slipped into our hiding place and we left. At the estuary, German customs officers inspected the boat. I could hear their boots and felt as if they were stomping on my heart. I was lying on my back and I held my baby in my arms. If he had uttered a cry, a moan, we were lost. I was talking in his ear and I'm sure that he understood. The visit was long. He had not emitted the slightest sound.

"When we settled in London, I paged through a kind of diary that my eldest keeps with great regularity. She had written well of waking in the night, praying, and my warnings. She concluded: 'For we who are accustomed to these things, we were not surprised.'"

Mathilde's first operation.

One of our most useful group leaders had recently been transported from the prison where he was detained to a hospital. Last night, an ambulance with four German soldiers and a nurse showed an order from the Gestapo to hand our sector boss over to her. Neither Mathilde nor her men had to use their weapons.

Félix, Lemasque, and Jean-François are working hard to organize a few mountain shelters where deserters have taken refuge to avoid deportation.

Visited Lemasque's sector.

I'm not emotional, but what I've seen, I don't believe I'll ever forget it. Hundreds and hundreds of young people returning to states of savagery. They can't wash. They can't shave. Their long hair dangles over cheeks burned by sun & rain. They sleep in holes, in caves, in mud. Food is a daily and terrible problem. Farmers do what they can, but that cannot last indefinitely. Their clothes are going to shreds. Their shoes are torn to pieces by stones. I saw boys with shoes made of pieces of old tires, or even pieces of bark attached to their feet with string. I saw others who had no other clothing than an old potato sack split in two and tied round their waist like a loincloth. It's becoming impossible to recognize where those boys come from. Are they farmers, workers, clerks, students? They all have the same gauntness, the same misery, the same hardness, and the same anger on their faces. The ones I visited were well disciplined by Lemasque & the helpers he had chosen. We get as much food and money as we can. But in the various maquis there are thousands of refugees. No secret organization can tend to their most elementary needs. Will they then die of hunger, take to looting, or surrender? And winter has not yet come. Woe to those who forced our young men to make such a choice!

———

Lemasque has improved in an astonishing way. The duties that he was in charge of when I was in London, his current position, taught him decisiveness, authority. He controls his nerves. His subdued enthusiasm has a certain and powerful affect on the kind of instinctive people he commands.

I don't have the time to see Jean-François and Félix's regions. I have to make an urgent report to London about this inspection by the next delivery.

––––––––

Félix has sent me a liaison agent with a whole list of things needed in his maquis. At the bottom of his list, the following note:

"Vichy had sent a company of *gardes mobiles* to the region to track us. I made contact with the captain. We talked things over. We came to an understanding. He told me: 'Have no fear. I was an officer of the Republican Guard. I took an oath to defend the Republic. Today the Republic is in the maquis. I defend it.'"

––––––––

Mathilde has made a discovery that definitively confirms some information we were not quite sure of.

The seamstress from whom Mathilde rented a garret has a son of more than 12 years old. Like all city children of our time, he has a grey complexion, flabby muscles, and famished eyes. He is very gentle and has a great delicacy of feeling. Mathilde loves him a lot. This little kid works as a bellboy at Hotel T. The job is good. Not so much for the salary but for the scraps that the child sometimes gets from the restaurant. Mathilde was invited to share some of those feasts. It appears that nothing is so pathetic as to see the little tyke pretend that he's not hungry so as to give as much as possible to his mother, & the mother plays the same comedy when neither can take their eyes off of the food.

But for some time the child spent terrible nights. He moaned, cried, screamed, gagged in his sleep. The shivering fits that seized him were almost convulsive. He seemed delirious. "Do no harm!…" "Don't kill her!…" "Stop, please, stop screaming like that!"

The mother sought advice from Mathilde, who she still takes for a nurse. Mathilde spent part of the night listening to the little one's nightmares. Then she woke him gently. She asked him questions. A woman who has had as many children as she and who loves them so much knows how to talk to them. The seamstress' son told her everything. About a week ago, he was put at the disposal of the guests who occupy the fourth floor of the hotel where he works. He must stand on the landing and respond to the bell. The whole floor is occupied by ladies and gentlemen, he said, speaking French well, but all of them are Germans. They receive many people. There are men and women who are always accompanied by two German soldiers. And the Frenchmen and the French women always look as if they were afraid but don't want to show it. And they are always taken to the same room, 87. Almost always screams and the noise of beatings and cries can be heard in that room. It stops and then resumes again and again. "Till it makes you sick, I swear to you, Madame," the child said to Mathilde. "The voices of the women they are harming, that especially is terrible. And if you could see the state they're in when they come out of there. Often they take them into another room & then they are brought back. It starts again. I didn't want to tell anyone because I'm afraid to think about it."

And that's how we'd located the torture chamber for that city.

———————

The following day Mathilde asked what advice I would have given the seamstress about her son.

— Get him out of the hotel immediately, I said.

— Eh, well, I persuaded the woman to let him stay on, Mathilde told me. It's so valuable to have a spy in such a place, and an innocent spy.

Mathilde's lips contracted and she gave me a very sad, interrogative look. I had been forced to tell her she was right.

———————

A severe blow for our newspaper.

It was set up at several different printers'. A part in each of them. Then the typographers working for us could work fast & not be noticed. Then, the leads were carried the same day to a mailbox that stood among ten others in a row in a hallway. The comrade who lived in the house and used the mailbox would take the leads and send them to another printing press where the newspaper is made. Yesterday the bottom of the mailbox, too old, no doubt, collapsed. The leads fell in the hallway. A foolish tenant passing by thought that they were explosives (almost every day there's a bomb attack in the city). The tenant notified the police. Our friend is in a cell. The Gestapo have already come for him.

I think that he will resist room 87. But in any case we have to change all the printing presses. Now, with the German tortures, we must observe strict rules. As soon as a comrade who knows something is arrested, it must be assumed *a priori* that everything that he knows, the Gestapo also knows. I change my name and address.

The captain of the *gardes mobiles* has kept the promise he made to Félix. He hasn't found a single deserter from deportation in the maquis. He conducts a round of the woods and valleys every day, but he takes care to send on reconnaissance a motorcyclist who makes an infernal racket. Then everyone is warned. But the captain has just advised Félix that two S.S. officers have arrived to supervise and direct the manhunt operations.

The owner of a brothel said to a friend who runs a bar:

— My house was requisitioned by the krauts. It's never worked so hard. But I don't want this money. It burns my hands. I'd like to use it against the krauts.

The bar owner has spoken of this desire to the Bison. The latter told this to Mathilde. She saw the brothel owner.

— "How will I know that it is really being used against the krauts?" the latter asked. "On the radio from London we'll broadcast an agreed upon sentence," said Mathilde. We'd given the sentence. It was repeated by the B.B.C. We received 500,000 francs. Additionally, the brothel owner has put a wonderful estate at our disposal. An old general who has helped us a lot through his military connections and who is being hunted by the police has already taken refuge there.

An experience of Félix's.

The captain of the *gardes mobiles* gave warning that the two S.S. officers were beginning to suspect his trick & that he would not be able to resist their pressure much longer. Félix began studying their haunts and habits. The company of the *gardes mobiles* is confined to a large village. The two Germans have rented a chalet on the side of the mountain. Waking very early, they always take their coffee in a small inn located between their chalet & the village. The trail leading to the inn has very steep slopes on both sides & at one point takes a sharp bend. The place is perfect for an ambush.

Félix has a machine gun. He could liquidate the Germans all by himself. But there are two stout guys in the village who say that they are willing to do anything against the krauts. One is the postman, the other the saddler. Félix thinks it's an opportunity to test them. If they are just café braggarts, it's better to be forewarned. If they are really capable of action, they must be brought into the fold. Félix offers the task to the postman and the saddler. They accept.

At dawn, the three men are at the bend in the path. Félix has his machine gun. The postman and the saddler have revolvers. The sun begins to rise. The Germans approach. They are heard talking and laughing loudly. They have no cares. They are masters in a conquered country. Félix appears and flashes his gun at them. The two officers watch for a second this short, bearded man, his round and red face. They raise their arms.

— They understood right away, said Félix, their faces did not even move.

Félix only had to pull the trigger to bury them. But he wanted the postman and the saddler to prove their mettle and pass their apprenticeship. He ordered each of them to kill a man. They came forward and fired several bullets, closing their eyes a little, it seemed. The Germans fell with great simplicity. Their grave was prepared in advance. Félix & his accomplices threw the bodies in & covered them with earth & grass. No one but those three men will ever be able to find the corpses of those S.S. officers.

— "It was beautiful work," Félix told me, "but to be frank, I was a little sick at heart. Those bastards had real courage. And that look when they realized what was up, I was hit in the guts. We hid our weapons and those of the S.S. and went & had coffee in the bistro where the krauts were going.

I wondered how my postman and saddler would react, because I, after all, who've seen hard times, still felt sick. Eh, well, them, they took their juice quietly and they started to snore on the bench. In the afternoon the postman carried his letters and the other sold his stuff like it was nothing."

Félix rubbed his tonsure and he said: "They've certainly changed, the French."

The boss will be delighted by the postman and the saddler. This man of exceptional intelligence and culture likes stories about children and simple people.

I stay with a young family of very modest means. The husband is an accountant for a silk merchant and spends his nights traveling as a liaison agent for us. His wife goes to the lines, cooks, takes care of the house, and serves as my secretary, which pushes her to spend sleepless nights, too. She faints rather frequently. I talk to the husband. He finds it natural. But he loves his wife. Yet our work comes first.

I believe that among the people of the resistance, an evolution is in process where they develop the inverse aspect of their temperaments. Those who were sweet, tender, peaceful, they become hard. Those who were as hard as I was, as I still am, become more permeable to feelings. The explanation? Perhaps the people who saw life in glowing colors defend themselves with a kind of inner shield when coming into contact with the often dreadful realities they discover in the resistance. And perhaps people like myself, who have a rather pessimistic view of mankind, discover through the resistance that man is much better than what they thought of him.

The boss alone still remains true to himself. I think that he has long since accepted the possibilities of good & evil which each human being unconsciously carries within himself.

Long conversation with Louis H, the leader of a group with which we often work. We first talked about a very specific matter. Louis H has three men in a French concentration camp, men whom he highly values. The Gestapo has requested those three men. They will be delivered to them by train in four days. Louis H's organization has been terribly tested in the last month & he doesn't have the resources to try to free his comrades. He came to ask me if we could take over the operation. I shall give the necessary orders.

Then, unwittingly, and as old high school, regiment, or war comrades do, we let ourselves fall into reminiscences. Both of us are veterans of the resistance. We have seen much water and blood run under the bridges. Louis H calculates that of the four hundred members who formed their original group, only five are still alive or at large. If we have a greater proportion of survivors (a question of luck, of organization, perhaps), the loss is nevertheless terrible. And the Gestapo mowing down without cease, closer, harder. But the enemy can no longer succeed in suppressing the resistance. It's over; it's too late. Louis H and I decided that if one year ago, if the Germans had shot or arrested a thousand well-chosen men, they would have beheaded our groups and divided the resistance for a long time to come, perhaps until the end of the war. Today, it is impossible. There are too many cadres, sub-cadres, volunteers, accomplices. Even if they deport all the men, the women would remain. And there are some astonishing ones. The resistance has taken the form of a Hydra. Cut off its head, ten more reemerge in its place, with each spurt of blood.

After Louis H leaves, I suffer a kind of depression. It isn't good to count the missing. And since then, for a long time, I haven't been sleeping enough. I think of Mont Valerian where *every day* men are shot, of that Chaville estate, where *every day* a truck brings convicted men to face a firing squad, of the shooting range of Z where *every day* our comrades are gunned down.

I thought of the cells of Fresnes, of the cellars of Vichy, of room 87 of Hotel T where every day, every night, they burn women's breasts, break toes, push pins under nails, send electrical currents through their genitals. I thought of prisons, of concentration camps where people are dying of hunger, of tuberculosis, of cold, of vermin. I have thought of our newspaper team, completely built from scratch three times over. Of sectors where not a man, not a woman remains of those who were there from the start.

And I asked myself in a positive spirit, like an engineer who makes a blueprint: Do the results that we are able to obtain justify those massacres? Is our newspaper worth the death of its editors, its printers, its distributors? Do our little sabotages, our detailed attacks, our humble secret army that will perhaps never act, does that outweigh our frightful devastations? Are we, the leaders, justified in arousing, training, and sacrificing so many brave people, and of those brave people, so many trusting, impatient, and exalted souls in blistering combat, in a struggle of secrets, famine, and torture? Are we, finally, really needed for victory?

In a positive spirit, as an honest mathematician, I had to admit that I didn't know. And even that I didn't believe it. Numerically, accounting practically, we are running at a loss. So, I thought, then we must honestly give up. But at the same time, when the thought of giving up came to me, I felt that it was impossible. Impossible to leave others the responsibility and the whole weight of defending us, of saving us. Impossible to leave the Germans with the memory of a country unable to jolt back into life, without dignity, without hatred. I felt that an enemy killed by us, who have neither uniform nor flag nor territory, I felt that the corpse of that enemy weighed more heavily, more effectively, in the scales that hold the fate of nations than a whole mass grave on a battlefield. I realized that we were waging the most glorious war of the French people. A war of little material use since victory is assured us even without our help. A war that nobody forces us into. A war without glory. A war of executions and attacks. A gratuitous war in a word. But this war is an act of hatred and an act of love. An act of life.

— "For a people to be so generous with its blood," said the boss one day with his silent laugh, "proves at least that they have red blood cells."

———————

A Communist girl said to me:

— A friend of mine, a little woman of no consequence, was so severely tortured at Santé that, after having escaped, she always has poison on her. You see, she couldn't begin to suffer that again. She would rather die. So she asked the party for poison in case she might be taken again. Because, to give up work against the krauts, you see, is out of the question. *One might as well die now.*

———————

Spent the day in the country with the owner of a large vineyard.

Among other things he said to me:

— The day you need a tank, let me know.

I learned that during the retreat of our armies he had picked up an old Renault tank. He had driven it into one of his garages and walled it up. I didn't have the courage to tell this man that his old scrap was good for nothing. He was so proud of it. And besides, he had risked his easy and smooth life for it.

Mathilde and the Bison left to arrange the escape of the three prisoners Louis H entrusted to us.

An adventure of Jean-François.

The region of the maquis where Jean-François works is not very far from a sizable city. He often goes there for provisions, liaisons, fake mission orders, etc. He went there too often, I think, because he was arrested when he got off the train. By the French police.

Having worked in the *Corps Francs*, Jean-François kept his taste for grenades. There were three in his suitcase. As he and his two guards advanced with the crowd of passengers through the narrow exit of the station, he was able to undo the latch of his suitcase and dump the contents on the ground. When picking up his things, he slipped the grenades into his pockets. As he was being taken to the commissariat, he knelt down twice to retie the laces of his shoes. The grenades were left in the gutter.

At that moment the police grew suspicious of his movements and cuffed him.

— Take them off for a moment so that he can sign his deposition, said the commissaire when Jean-François was brought before him. Hardly had the handcuffs been removed when Jean-François relaxed his arms then swiftly struck the officers on either side of him. As they fell, they clung to Jean-François. He shook free of them, pushed the commissaire backwards, then ran toward the exit of the police station. A priest entered at that moment.

— Thief!… thief… shouted the officers who had gone in pursuit of Jean-François. The priest blocked the doorway.

— Gaullist! Gaullist!… bellowed Jean-François.

The priest let him pass and immediately blocked the way for the officers. They tumbled together in the doorway. While the officers disentangled themselves from the priest's cassock, Jean-François turned down one street, then another, then yet another, and found himself free of their clutches.

But for how long? They had his description. His jacket had been torn in the scuffle. If he went to someone he knew, he could put the police on the trail of the whole local organization. He had to leave town quickly. But the train station was monitored more closely than any other place. Jean-François decided to go on foot, but first he had to change his appearance. He went into a barbershop. It was empty. He called for the owner. A man came out of the back room, shuffling in his slippers. He had a sly, unpleasant face, with cautious, beady eyes hidden behind flabby eyelids. The head of a real informer. But Jean-François had neither time nor alternative. He explained that he wanted his mustache shaved off and for his naturally ash-blonde hair to be dyed black.

— A joke I'm going to play. A bet with a girlfriend, he said.

The barber said nothing. He goes to work in silence. From time to time, in the mirror, Jean-François seeks the gaze of the barber. He never finds it. They did not exchange a single word for a whole hour.

— I'm done for, Jean-François was thinking.

— How's that? the barber finally asked.

— Very nice, said Jean-François.

He was in fact quite unrecognizable. His hard, dark face was even painful for him to look at. He gave the barber twenty francs.

— I'll bring you change, said the latter.

— Never mind, said Jean-François.

— I'll bring you change, the barber repeated.

He disappeared behind a very dirty curtain. Jean-François was so sure of being denounced that he hesitated between two getaways — simply flee, or whack the guy and then flee. He had no time to decide. The barber came back almost immediately with an old raincoat over his arm.

— Put this on quickly, he said in a low voice and without looking at Jean-François. The coat is no beauty, but it's the only one I've got. You'll be spotted with torn clothes like yours.

Jean-François recounts that adventure gaily, as always, but that gaiety did not seem to have its usual freshness. The laughter is a little hardened. It is perhaps his blackened hair that changes the entirety of his expressions. Or perhaps he too began to carry the mark of a perpetually endangered man & to feel the invisible presence always lurking behind his shoulders. In any case, he will no longer meet with the boss.

I don't want the least thread to lead the police to Saint Luc. I said that to Jean-François. He agreed and said nothing. He rarely talks about his brother, and when he does, it's very brief. The fact that his brother & the boss are the same person seems to bewilder him. I regret Jean-François' reserve — I used to very much like to hear him say "Saint Luc."

The three comrades with whose escape Louis H has entrusted us took the train yesterday at 7:45 A.M. They were in a third-class compartment, handcuffed and guarded by five gendarmes. Mathilde got on the train at the same time. She wore a black coat and a scarf of the same color on her head. She ended up in the same car as the prisoners. The train went through several stations, then sped through a deserted countryside. At 11:10 A.M., Mathilde set off the alarm. Then she crept into the compartment adjoining the prisoners' & stood close to the door and undid her black shawl. A few moments later, as the train was coming to a stop, the Bison and two of our men emerged from behind the railway embankment &

entered the compartment where the gendarmes and Louis H's comrades were. Our men had submachine guns. The gendarmes removed the handcuffs from the prisoners. Then we made the gendarmes undress. They didn't seem too upset. Louis H's comrades and our men took the uniforms of the gendarmes and their musketoons and jumped on the track. The conductor arrived at that moment.

— You can go, the Bison exclaimed to him. The train started moving again. Mathilde didn't even get out.

———

The place chosen for the kidnapping is about twelve kilometers from a fairly large estate. The property belongs to the big vintner who offered me the tank. He was hiding on the other side of the embankment of the railway line with a cart and two horses. In the cart there were large empty barrels. Louis H's men and ours hid in the bottom of the barrels. The vintner brought them to the cellar of his house. The Bison and his two comrades left at nightfall. The escaped prisoners will hole up at the vintner's for a week. And be fattened up.

———

In the course of a trip down their way I spent an evening with them. The three men hardly have any flesh left on their bones. The discipline of the camp was much more severe than at the one where I had met Legrain. Hard & stupid work. No mail.

Constant surveillance. Night watchmen in every barrack. A high-voltage current in the barbed wire. The prisoners were so famished that they ate the grass that grew in the camp. The commandant made his inspection every morning with a bullwhip under his arm. That set the temperature for the guards.

— However, brutalities had suddenly ceased thanks to the intervention of the most impertinent of our comrades, said one of the escapees. In normal times this country squire spent his hours composing adventure stories that were published in local papers. He carried on the resistance in the style of his stories. The miracle is that he has not been shot. We have never seen a more impulsive, prolix, chimerical man. But one day he told the commandant that he had a radio transmitter hidden in the camp. That he communicated with London & that he would have the commandant executed if another inmate was struck even once more. And the old brute was scared.

In the same camp there was a section for communists. As always they were treated in a particularly appalling way. Somehow a few of them managed to escape. Three days later they voluntarily returned as prisoners. They had escaped *without the party's authorization.* The party sent them back to the camp.

This fact reminds me of a conversation I had with a communist deputy who had escaped from the Châteaubriant camp. He could easily escape. He would not do so before his party commanded him to. Only three of his comrades were designated to make the escape. The others remained. They were subsequently included in the first official massacre of hostages.

In prison and at the concentration camp, the cruelest torment that this deputy could think of was that he was to be taken prisoner in his home — because the Communist Party had ordered its official militants never to sleep at home.

— You understand, said this man who had given twenty-five years of his life to the party, you understand, I could be expelled. And I would have deserved it. Fortunately, the executive committee was lenient. They simply gave me a good dressing down & put me to work.

This work consisted in editing the clandestine magazine *Humanité*. At the time, four of its chief editors had already been shot one after the other.

I don't know of a man in the resistance who doesn't speak of the communists with a special quality in his voice and face. A deeper gravity.

An officer from the French headquarters in London came to spend a few weeks in Paris on an important mission. In the metro, the day after the bombing of the Renault factories by the Americans, we heard a worker from the same factory, and who had his arm in a sling, openly gloating about the results of the raid. My companion slipped something into the worker's good hand. It was the Cross of Lorraine.

— I well know that that gesture was stupid, my companion then told me, but I haven't been in France for three years. The discovery of this new people makes my head turn a bit.

———

Long journey in the company of Commandant Marquis de B.

Sentenced to hard labor for life for his patriotism, he escaped after thirty months of horrible imprisonment. He is a man of exceptional temperament, extremely daring, and always lucid. While waiting to find passage to England, he traveled the country in every direction to gather information, as if his life was normal, and as if all the police were not searching for him.

— I have the feeling that I've been living as a blind man, he said. In my circle, we had neither the opportunity nor the time nor the inclination, it must be said, to get close to and to know the people. Since my escape, I've seen only them. I won't forget the lesson.

One evening, through a hitch in the liaisons, Commandant de B found himself without papers & without money, in a village where he knew no one. He knocked on a teacher's door & asked for hospitality. Without asking any questions, the teacher led this stranger into his dining room where dinner — naturally pitiful — was being served. There was a woman & two children. After the meal, Commandant de B took the teacher aside and said to him:

— You have a family. I must warn you that I am a senior officer of General de Gaulle's, an escapee, & that the Gestapo has put a price on my head.

The teacher lifted up a floorboard and showed the major two parabellums.

———

When changing trains, we found a place in a compartment where there was a very drunk German soldier. He soon began vomiting on our feet. The face of Commandant de B became very pale, & he said in a low voice: "*Heraus, Schwein …*" Did the soldier believe he was in the presence of a German officer in plainclothes or a Gestapo agent? Did he simply automatically obey an imperious voice? I don't know. But he left the compartment.

———

Many people of the resistance spend the majority of their time on trains. Nothing can be trusted to telephones, telegrams, or letters. All mail must be carried. Every confidence, every contact, requires a journey. And there is the distribution of weapons, newspapers, transmitters, sabotage equipment.

This explains the need for an army of liaison agents who move through France like carousel horses. This also explains the terrible blows that they suffer. The enemy knows as well as we do the necessity of our constant movement. I have never taken a trip of any length without encountering two, three, four comrades from my organization or another. And I sussed out many more whom I did not know. Being a conspirator leads to developing an almost infallible instinct in that respect. I wonder if that instinct is as strong in police officers.

———

I believe that I am being followed by a genteel old man with a manicured beard who is a legionnaire. A head-on maneuver of the Gestapo? I'm having some of our guys trail the old fellow.

———

The Bison had a stupid accident. He was riding very fast on a motorcycle stolen from the Germans and skidded. Coma. Hospital. He was carrying two revolvers and a switchblade.

The weapons were deposited at the Registry. The French and German police were notified. They carried the still unconscious Bison to an operating table. Fractured skull, broken jaw. They treat him. The police arrive but because he was still unconscious they put off the frisking and questioning till the following night. The Bison returns to his senses at dawn.

His head is completely wrapped in bandages. He suffers terribly. No guards. He gets up and leaves the hospital through a window. He staggers through the town. A tramway passes which goes toward a suburb where he has friends. He enters the tram.

— I could see four doors, the Bison said afterwards. Luckily I found the right one.

There are two people following me. The old legionnaire and another who pretends to sell tickets for the National Lottery. I must vanish. I have undoubtedly been traveling too much.

It's very unpleasant. The woman who hides me is riddled with fear. A priest who is working with us asked her to shelter me. She did it out of a sense of duty and because this priest has been her spiritual guide for years. But I sense constant anguish. If someone rings or knocks, her breathing stops, & yet it is impossible for me to remain without liaisons.

I dream up disguises. But I have eyes that are too close together, a characteristic nose. The beard on my face is unnatural & the police are now suspicious of all beards. I'm not cut out to be an actor. We had a comrade who could easily transform himself into a hunchback. He looked so pitiful that the Germans often gave their place to him in the metro. He sat with a thousand precautions. He carried many things in his hump.

———

An urgent mission obliges me to travel. What a relief in the eyes of the woman who has been harboring me!

———

The same day that I left Mme. S's apartment, the police came. The search yielded nothing. They took Mme. S away all the same.

———

I went away to complete a series of plans which I have been preparing for a long time and which London is interested in. Ordinarily, I stay with a farmer who lives close enough to my target and who gives me all the information. So as not to be noticed in this region that is under heavy surveillance, a doctor from the city takes me by car to a clearing where I succeed in reaching the farm under cover of the bushes. This time the doctor was short of gasoline. He was only able to bring me to a sunken path and then left immediately. At the entrance — it was beautiful evening — a German soldier was strolling about. He didn't see me get out but he saw the car come & go.

I dined with the farmer. I showed him my recent plans. And just as I'd slipped them back into my pocket, the soldier I'd seen on the sunken path entered and gestured to me to follow him. The path was deserted. I thought for a moment of leaping on his back, gouging his eyes out, & doing him in. But I was afraid of getting the farmer shot. That is also the reason why I did not dare dispose of my plans. We had arrived at a military post. The soldier took me to the lieutenant in command & explained my case. This lieutenant was dark & I remember very well that that face gave me hope. I prefer dark to fair Germans.

— What were you doing at that farmer's place? the lieutenant asked me. I had had time to prepare my response. I said I was an agricultural insurance broker.

— What company?

— The Zurich, I said. I didn't think of it randomly. I don't know what impulse warned me that if any insurance company name was capable of interesting the officer, and thereby disarming his suspicion, that was the one. And indeed, he knew the city of Zurich & so did I. We spoke of its gardens, its theaters, its museums. And of Switzerland. And he let me go without searching me.

The plans that I had taken were to be handed over by me to a large business office in Paris, on Avenue de l'Opéra.

Two days later, having traveled solely by small local lines, I headed there to present myself. As I was about to ring, the door opened of its own accord. A hand gently took me by the wrist & drew me inside. I found myself in the presence of German policemen. Since morning the office had become a mousetrap.

— Who are you? What have you come here to do?

I invent a motive consistent with the normal operations of the business.

— Papers.

I show them the latest ones, which were fabricated after my having been shadowed by the two old men. One of the policemen went to the telephone and spoke with one of the Gestapo bases. I understand German. I follow the conversation. At the other end of the line they asked the officer to read a list of names. I heard the one that I went under just ten days ago. The officer turned back to me, gave me my papers, pushed me to the door. I tried to go down as slowly as I could. In the concierge's lodge, I thought I saw a man with glasses. I go out, I walk, and I stop before a storefront. A few paces from me is the man with glasses. I go to a bakery that I know. It has a double exit. I thereby gain a few minutes. I see a fire station. I find some well-disposed people. They hide me in a fire truck and take me to a junk shop on the Left Bank, one of our best agents. I entrust my plans to him & leave Paris the day after, pushing a handcart full of old chairs.

Three times, in quick succession, I escaped the worst. Extraordinary combination of probabilities. A believer would have called that streak a succession of miracles. A baccarat player would have said it was a good hand.

———————

I go into hiding in a tiny village at the house of a clandestine butcher. Each day brings him a pig, or a calf, or a sheep, which he bleeds, slaughters, & chops up. He is protected by the entire population, which he feeds with cheap meat. This man is a saint of the black market. He wants no more than to make a living. His pleasure is in playing with the Germans, playing with Vichy. He fed me and put me up at a ridiculous price. He gives me the best pieces. I am saturated with meat, which is a marvel. He also hides a former minister who must soon leave for London. We play pétanque together. The weather is lovely. The mountain air is bracing. Time passes.

———————

When one goes, as we do, from one precarious refuge to another, at the mercy of accomplices, good will or pursuit, one is bound to visit some unique places. The faculty for astonishment wanes. But this time mine is entirely awakened by a new refuge.

It is a small 18th-century manor, with wainscoting, tapestries, paintings, and furniture from the period. All around, silent high forests. Before the façade, a pond with blooming water lilies. The alleys are overgrown with moss. Everything seems to be asleep within this estate whose perimeters are lined with crumbling walls.

The manor belongs to two old ladies, two sisters who have never married. They have lived here for three-quarters of a century. They had a brother whom they adored. He was killed in 1914. Their friends died out gradually. They know no one. The property lies far from the roads. They have never seen a German. Their food, which consists of vegetables and dairy products, has not changed. An old farmer supplies them. The world & life have forgotten these women.

My clandestine butcher would see the farmer from time to time. He spoke to him about me. The farmer spoke of me to the two women. And here I am.

During the day I walk among the enchanted forest where animals have no fear of man. In the evening, I listen to the song of frogs, and later, to the cry of the Eurasian eagle owls. At mealtimes, the old ladies, in exquisite language, ask me questions about the war. But they cannot follow my explications. They are ignorant of airplanes, tanks, radios, even of phones. They were already sunk in a kind of lethargy when another war began. The death of their brother definitively stopped the course of the universe for them. The only war that, for them, is real and living is the war of 1870. Their father, uncles, & older cousins took part in it. The stories they had collected about it gave an aura of excitement to the youth of these two women. Their hatred of the Prussians goes back to a time when I was not yet born.

Once, I tried to depict some of the traits of the resistance to the old ladies. They nodded their slender, wrinkled heads:

— I see, I see, my sister, said one of them to the other.

— They are like the *francs-tireurs*.

— But decent and well-mannered, my sister, cried the other again.

———

Time passes. Time weighs heavy. I think often of the boss. He could live indefinitely in a place like this. I wish I had his book. The only one he has written. Few people know it. But several scholars throughout the world hold J for their equal because of this book. And because of it, I wanted to know him. For a long time he has been my spiritual master.

———

Time passes.

I amuse myself by drawing from memory the list of clandestine newspapers that I know:

L'Avant-Garde
L'Art Français
Bir-Hakeim
Combat
L'École Laïque
L'Enchaîné du Nord

L'Étudiant patriote

France d'abord

Franc-Tireur

Le Franc-Tireur Normand

Le Franc-Tireur Parisien

L'Humanité

L'Insurgé

Les Lettres Françaises

Libération

Libérer et Fédérer

Le Médecin Français

Musiciens d'aujourd'hui

Pantagruel

Le Père Duchesne

Le Piston

Le Populaire

Résistance

Rouge Midi

Russie d'aujourd'hui

L'Université Libre

Valmy

La Vie Ouvrière

La Voix du Nord

La Voix de Paris

La Voix Populaire

There was also *La Voix des Stalags*.

In early 1942, several Parisian prisoners of war met in Paris, some freed due to their poor health, most others having escaped. They spoke of life in the camps and everyone agreed that it would be good to distribute among the prisoners a paper that would counteract the propaganda circulated among them in favor of Marshal Pétain & which the Germans encourage in every way.

The reunited comrades decided to publish *La Voix des Stalags*. They found the paper and the printer. They wrote the articles and the news items. But in what form could the newspaper be realized? Merchants were giving enough supplies to make up hundreds of packages to conceal the thin sheets. But how could they prevent the packages from being searched, and how obtain the necessary addresses?

One member of the committee solved both problems at once. He went to the office of *Je suis partout* and told an employee the following story:

He was the principal of a school. He had set up a regular collection system among his pupils to send gifts to prisoners. He had been a prisoner himself and, in Germany, he had read with enthusiasm the virulent collaborationist campaigns carried out by *Je suis partout*. Also, he would like to publicize the paper among the prisoners.

The faux school principal was eagerly taken to the editor-in-chief. He obtained 1,200 addresses in the different Stalags, printed on labels of the journal that works on behalf of the enemy. There was no better safe conduct for *La Voix des Stalags*.

———————

I have a new name and I have newly shaved my mustache. My hair is very long and I wear an old cape. I am the accountant of an industrial magnate who employs a hundred workers. I sleep at the factory. The most regular ID card is no longer good enough for the police. During my retreat, the control machine, the machine for stifling us, tightened its grip with great force. Because of the deportations and the deserters, they demand a work permit, a census certificate, and a residence certificate. The raids and the battering continue mercilessly. They search trams, restaurants, cafés, cinemas. They purge entire neighborhoods apartment by apartment. It's difficult to go even one hundred kilometers on a train without being questioned by the police.

The job becomes hellish. Women will have more & more work.

———————

Rent an atelier for our contacts.

In this place I pass for an artist who paints when he desires or who entertains his comrades.

———————

This morning, I had an appointment at the atelier with Jean-François, Lemasque, & Félix. I hadn't seen them for months.

We need to fix many things for their maquis. As I was approaching the place, the concierge was on the doorstep feebly beating an old rug. Seeing me cross the street, she suddenly began to frantically beat the doormat. She had never been one of us; she knows nothing of our activity. However I did not enter.

———

That woman had deliberately saved my life. An extremely simple chain of circumstances has led to a catastrophe.

When leaving the region, Jean-François delegated his command to an ex-officer who has great authority but too much optimism and no conspiratorial wit. He needed to deliver a message to Jean-François and he sent him a liaison agent. He chose a very young boy devoid of experience. Instead of using a relay point, he gave him the street address and atelier number. The boy, while waiting for a connecting train, fell asleep. He was awakened by a raid. They found my address on him. He had failed to invent a plausible explanation. Mousetrap. Lemasque, Félix, and Jean-François were taken. The concierge had thought then of that means of warning: the doormat.

———

News about Jean-François.

Having before him all the reports he found on Jean-François, Lemasque, & Félix, the *commissaire* questioned him in the atelier. Jean-François said nothing of importance. Suddenly, he bit the *commissaire* on the hand, and so hard that he tore off a piece of his palm. He grabbed the documents, slammed the two inspectors against one another, and burst down the stairs. He sent me the reports and returned to the maquis with my instructions.

News about Félix.

On a thin piece of paper, Félix had the address of an emergency apartment in the name of a young girl, which is where I would sometimes go, disguised as a security guard. Félix had written this address in a code of his own. When questioned, he was able to interpret the code as an appointment made on a certain day and at a certain hour in a public square with an important leader of the resistance. He did so with hesitation, evasions, and a reticence that was made to be taken for truth. And in the same way he agreed to lead two policemen in such a way that it would be believed.

Félix arrived in the middle of the square. He preceded the police by a few paces. A tramway was passing. He jumped in, ran through it, exited from the other side, and disappeared among the crowd.

Félix then wanted to warn me and went to the emergency address. Yet, in the meantime, the girl who had rented it came to the atelier and the police had managed to make her talk. Félix was taken again.

He is locked up like Lemasque in Vichy, in the cellars of Hotel Bellevue, which has been requisitioned by the Gestapo.

———————

In the factory I saw a young worker who spent eight months without reason in the German quarter of Fresnes prison. He has two broken ribs & limps for life.

What's most unbearable in his opinion is the strong odor of pus that has spurted onto the cell walls.

— The smell of our tortured friends, he said.

I think of Lemasque. I think of my old Félix.

———————

News about Lemasque.

He was locked up in the same cellar as Félix. He was in handcuffs and leg irons. Félix was considered the more dangerous. They were furious with him for having deceived the Gestapo. They questioned him from day one. He didn't return from the interrogation. But that night, by the brightness of the ceiling lights, Lemasque saw Félix's corpse being dragged through the corridor by a rope around his neck.

Félix had no eyes. Félix had no lower jaw. Lemasque recognized him mainly by the top of his bald head ... Félix la Tonsure.

Lemasque had such fear of undergoing the same tortures that suddenly he *knew* that he would escape.

Lemasque succeeds (he'll never be able to say how he got through) in undoing the padlock that fastened his ankles in irons. Night comes. With his chained hands, he loosens the weak bars of the cellar vent and, feet first, slips out. There he was on the streets of Vichy still handcuffed. The only person he knew there was a ministry clerk who lived in a requisitioned hotel. Lemasque had been to see him just once to obtain false mission orders. In streets overrun by patrols of *gardes mobiles* and Gestapo making their rounds, Lemasque, handcuffed, began to search for the hotel. He had to find it before dawn or he was done for. Hours pass. He kept wandering through Vichy. Finally, he thought he found the place. He entered the hotel. One last effort — a desperate attempt to remember the floor and the exact room. Lemasque finally seemed to remember. He knocked on the door. It opened. It was our comrade.

That evening, a friendly worker came with a hacksaw to free Lemasque of his handcuffs. I did confirm the story through the ministry clerk and the worker. Otherwise I'd always wondered if Lemasque hadn't weakened and invented this evasion on behalf of the Gestapo.

The resistance attacks, sabotages, and kills with abundance and persistence. Instinctively. All organizations have their fighting squads. The *francs-tireurs* form a real army. The density of German corpses has become such that the enemy has had to renounce the hostage system. They cannot continue to line up 100 dead Frenchman for one dead German. Or they would have to gun down the whole of France. The enemy has thus publically recognized that the country was triumphing over terror.

But the Gestapo continues its terrible work. It aims to replace hostages with suspects.

I'm taking charge of a reception. In my post I am not supposed to attend to operation details, but we had very high losses. There is no one left in the sector that can conduct a mission of this kind. Mathilde is coming with me; she will learn the craft. The group consists of a taxi owner, his wife, and a village blacksmith. They had been lent to us by Louis H's group. I don't know any of them.

We spent the first night on the ground without results.

For one hour a plane circled above us in the dark, but there was fog. The pilot probably could not see our light signals. At dawn we withdrew to a cabin. It belongs to the blacksmith who is also a poacher and who built it in a forest on the border of our territory. The taxi is parked under the trees, with a camouflaged transmitter. We exchanged messages with London. The plane will return the following night.

———

It rained till evening. We had nothing to eat, nothing to drink, and very little to smoke. I chattered with my group.

The taxi owner is a former aircraft mechanic. As soon as he was able to get in touch with people from the resistance, he made his gazogène and himself available. He worked a lot. He hasn't had a single accident. His sole adventure is rather special.

Last year, in the main cinema of the small town where he lives, three Germans were killed with a grenade. The *Kommandantur* made it known that the hostages would be shot. The French police commissaire, who belonged to no organization and who was simply a brave man, found the German *Kommandant* and protested that the incident in the theater was not an attack made by the resistance, but the wrath of soldiers returning from the Russia front against others who had never been there. The German officer listened attentively to the *commissaire* and offered him a deal:

— I will give you three days to prove what you claim. If you do not succeed, you will be shot, and with you a resident of the city who is willing to vouch for you.

The *commissaire* accepted. He talked it over with the taxi owner with whom he was friendly, though without knowing that the other belonged to a secret organization. The taxi owner accepted. Two days passed. On the third, the *commissaire* managed to collect irrefutable proof.

— It is perhaps because of this affair that I haven't yet had any hassle with the Gestapo, the taxi driver said to me. That gave me a first-class alibi. You understand. The Fritzes had never believed that an underground agent would risk such a blow. But at the time I didn't think about it, and for forty-eight hours I had paroxysms, I swear to you.

———

The taxi driver's wife is in her thirties. She is youthful, obliging, and motherly. She hates the Germans with a kind of inhuman innocence. She rejoices when bombs kill the children of the Rhineland. "The only good kraut," she said gently, "is a dead kraut."

One evening, during a reconnaissance mission within the vicinity of a German camp, the taxi driver's wife cut her knee on some barbed wire. She put a handkerchief around the wound, which was bleeding a lot, and reached the nearest train station. On the train she sat next to a German soldier. He saw the blood-soaked handkerchief. He had a sensitive heart. He insisted on replacing the handkerchief with his field bandage.

— While he was bandaging my leg I stared at the nape of his neck, the taxi driver's wife said to me.

— What a beautiful place for a thrust of the knife, lost! It was necessary nonetheless to do something against him. So, I stole his flashlight. Look, there it is. We use it for signals.

———

The poaching blacksmith is named — is this true? — Joseph Pioche. His face is the color of terracotta. Small laughing eyes. He has the lips of a man who loves good food and girls. Beneath his simple air, he is one of the finest and most resolute of men. He doesn't like speaking of his adventures. But they are famous among the comrades. The taxi driver forced him to recount some.

Pioche, who is a remarkable radio operator, had set up his station in a small house they'd rented in the fields. After some time, the region had become very unsafe. Tracking cars were cruising around. We had to change locales, but on the last day Pioche had to send twenty-two extremely important telegrams. Twenty-two telegrams take a very long time when you're surrounded by trackers. Pioche barricaded himself in the house with his two well-armed sons. They were instructed to hold out till all the messages were transmitted, but Pioche was able to transmit the telegrams without a hitch.

He had one, a bit later, in Paris. He was coming out of Gare de Lyon to deliver some forged seals and false stamps to a comrade when Doriot's men, who worked for the Germans, arrested him. They forced him into a car and took him to Fresnes. Pioche lit his pipe.

— That's certainly the last that you'll smoke, said one of the thugs that accompanied him. Pioche smoked and smoked quickly. And each time he put his hand in his tobacco pouch, he pulled out a stamp or a seal and slid it under the cushions. Then he said:

— If I must die soon, so much the better to eat the chicken that I have in my musette.

He bit into a thigh, he bit into a wing, and all the while his agile fingers searched the carcass, which was stuffed with seals and stamps and, along with the bones, he threw them out the window. When he reached Fresnes, he no longer had anything dangerous on him. Nonetheless, and to make him confess, they led him three times to the execution wall. He wept out of sheer innocence. In the end they released him. What amuses Pioche most in this case is the fact that in Fresnes he met a squire who had had him thrown into prison for poaching on his estate. They became good friends. The other had been shot.

———

Those stories held us over till dark without too much boredom. We went to the field. This time the signals were seen by the plane. It landed in exactly the right spot. The British airmen who perform these missions are first rate. But the plane was too heavy for the soaked ground.

It got stuck in the mud so deep that the united efforts of the crew, the passengers, and us could not pull the aircraft free. Then the British pilot said with magnificent confidence:

— We must get help from the neighboring village.

— Come with me to see the mayor, Pioche said to him, because, alone, he may not believe me.

They went to wake the mayor and returned with all the men of the village.

They freed the plane.

———

After his escape, Lemasque took only a week off then went right back to work. He has just been arrested again. Fortunately, he is for the moment still in the hands of the French police. Mathilde has promised me that she will get him out of prison. However, since Lemasque knows where I live, I change homes.

———

A little house of a retired official at the edge of a village. It's being rented by X, an old friend who is also hiding under a false identity.

His wife has been deported to Germany. Their son, a 10 year-old boy, is with him. In the evening, at dinner, I naturally call X by his real name and he, naturally, responds. The little boy nudges X with his elbow & whispers: "Duval, you see, Papa, we're Duval."

———

Mathilde, her hair hennaed and a pillow under her dress, posed as Lemasque's pregnant mistress. She has been granted permission to see him. Lemasque's escape was quite easy thanks to inside accomplices, on the condition that Lemasque's cellmate, a rather dubious character, be disposed of. Mathilde had slipped him a small vial for this. Lemasque refused to poison the man who is most probably a spy.

———

Mathilde gave Lemasque some chloroform. He refused to use it because he was afraid of miscalculating the dose. Time is running out though. The Gestapo will claim Lemasque. I think he still remembers Dounat.

———

This morning, a Sunday morning, I had a great scare. A German military car stopped in front of our house and a *Kommandant* got out. I was standing at the window. (Being unable to go out, I spend much of the day at this post.) And although I was hidden by a curtain, I recoiled. X's son, who was playing in the room, glanced into the street. "It's nothing," he said to me. "The region *Kommandant* comes to the corner bistro every Sunday. He thinks that they've the best Marc Morin of the country. If you continue to watch a bit, you'll have a good laugh. We'll keep watch together." The child had a mysterious air. After an hour, I saw the *Kommandant* go to the yard of the cafe and roll around in a pile of manure. "That isn't the kraut," the boy then said to me triumphantly.

"That's what happens. The *Kommandant* drinks a bottle of Morin. When he's good and well drunk, he insists upon changing clothes with the boss. And the disgusted boss will soil the kraut's uniform with manure." The child laughed silently and at first I did as him. But then I asked myself if at bottom the *Kommandant* did not hate his uniform and if, freed by alcohol, he was not covering it with filth by proxy.

The sensibility of the Germans sometimes manifests itself through the strangest of detours.

A young nurse whom I knew was assigned to tend to an S.S. captain. He was courting her. That made the young girl furious. "I like to see you angry," the S.S. captain said. "You're even prettier then."

"It's not difficult," replied the nurse, "I only have to see a kraut." And the captain was delighted. But often he would say:

"I should like to be a preacher with invincible speech and to have all the French at my feet. And you would embrace my knees."

Lemasque has been transferred to another prison. There, he found a comrade of ours who is very sick and very damaged by the interrogations. Mathilde had organized a getaway for the day when we had taken Lemasque for the last time from the prison to the examining magistrate. Everything was ready.

Our men were about to open fire. But Lemasque, who was holding up his comrade, signaled negative with his head to Mathilde and continued to brace his comrade, who was trailing along with difficulty. On leaving the Palais de Justice, both were handed over to the Gestapo. For a moment I was angry with Lemasque. But undoubtedly he has found his own Legrain?

Félix's wife begs to be allowed to work for us. She knew nothing of his underground activity. She learned of his downfall through an emissary of ours who was to give her relief but who had strict orders not to reveal any details about the organization: no relay, no reference point. Félix's wife refused the money and began to cry without screaming: "My poor man," she repeated. "If only I had known, if only I had known." She couldn't forgive herself for having reproached Félix so often for his absences, his apparent idleness.

I don't know how she managed to find one of us. From echelon to echelon her request finally reached Mathilde, who alone knows my refuge & who transmitted the request to me. Félix's wife will be a liaison agent. It's very dangerous work but the widows of executed comrades accomplish these tasks better than anyone.

We will take Félix's tuberculosis stricken little boy into our charge.

The question of children is heavy. There are hundreds & probably thousands who have neither father nor mother.

Shot, imprisoned, deported. I know of cases in which children had accompanied their parents to prison gates and who were kicked away by guards. I know of other cases where they've been left alone, abandoned in an apartment from where their parents had been seized. And other cases where the first thought of those children was to prowl around their empty houses so as to warn friends of the mousetrap.

I knew a woman who was crossing the border from Spain with soldiers and British airmen. She took them one by one, disguised as convalescents, playing the role of wife, presenting their papers, avoiding incidents. To complete the family setting, her seven-year-old son always accompanied her. She made the trip fifty-four times, then the ploy was discovered. They shot her. The child's fate is unknown.

———

Lemasque was taken to room 87. He fainted after half an hour of questioning. He regained consciousness. He swallowed a cyanide pill.

———

The most recent invention of the Gestapo interrogators — twisting a dental drill in the gum until the rowel strikes the jawbone.

———

I sent Mathilde and Jean-François to inspect our radio transmitters one by one. Or rather what's left of them.

We had a very bad streak.

At the beginning of the resistance, we could "tap" to London without too much risk. The Germans were not numerous enough to monitor clandestine broadcasts and had few tools. But at that time, we lacked transmitters, experienced operators, continuous liaisons with England. The work was done in a rather disorganized and primitive way. Today we are infinitely better equipped and trained. Only, as in every war, the enemy very quickly joined the parade. It has a first-class technical staff and detection cars, disguised as delivery, mail, or Red Cross trucks which patrol, prowl, and swarm, spying throughout the country.

I happened to observe one of those cars approaching its objective. It was creeping along, at the pace of a lingerer. Before each house it stopped for a second and went off again with supple muteness. One sensed that within the car some inexorable mechanism reduced its radius of approach meter by meter. One had the impression that a ruthless beast was feeling out the houses one after another and pushing its tentacles through the walls.

After it has caught the first waves, it doesn't take much more than half an hour for a car to find itself before the exact spot where a station operates. And half an hour is very short to make contact with London and to transmit messages. So we struggle. While the operator works, a comrade keeps watch at the window and another stands guard in the street.

Upon catching sight of the beast that is hot on its trail, the street lookout makes the agreed upon signal to the lookout in the window, who in turn warns the operator. It's a game of speed & luck. During the last week it's been unfavorable.

Ajax was taken completely by surprise. His lookouts were guarding the front of the house. The Gestapo came through a back alley. This time the detection device was hidden in a fire truck & it was by using a telescopic ladder that the German police came in through the window. Ajax avenged himself as he could. He asked his assistant: "But what's she done with the time bomb?" The Gestapo agents were very afraid. Ajax took the opportunity to destroy his transmission plan.

We have no details about Diamant's arrest. We only know that in the midst of a message to London, he suddenly tapped out: "Police … police … police …" and the broadcast was cut off.

———

It was Achilles that I loved the most. Before the war he served as a waiter in a popular restaurant where I sometimes went. A small, rather elderly man, dark and gentle. He took very well to the operator trade. He was exceptionally conscientious & skillful. He always managed to convey his messages. Even when the detection car was spotted he continued to tap. He knew just when to stop. He had an inner feel for seconds. Perhaps because he had been a waiter. He only had to be wrong once. He was shot the day after he was found out.

Received a report on a French family of average means. The eldest son, a landowner, bon vivant, and radical municipal councilor, is the vibrant spur of a whole information network. He had killed several Germans in raids. He's wanted and there's a price on his head. His wife is hiding in the woods of the region. His two brothers are group leaders in the maquis. The father, who for important business makes contact with the Germans in Paris, uses their relationship to smuggle arms, mail, transmitters, and to obtain valuable confidential information. The mother, who is aware of all of this activity, approves.

When a man of the resistance is taken on mere suspicion, he still has some chance of surviving, but if that man is a Jew, he is sure to die in the most atrocious way. Despite that there are many Jews in our organizations.

Mathilde has completed her inspection of the Augustine's farm, from which I left last year for Gibraltar. The operator, who is very young, had been a fool. His fiancée spent a few hours as the chief of a department. He took a train to see her.

He didn't return. He was surely picked up in a raid and sent, given his age, to Germany.

At the farm, Mathilde and Jean-François found messages to be transmitted that had been brought by liaison agents. There was a list and some were urgent. They studied the transmission plan & Jean-François, who is a good operator, began to tap.

The post was set up in one of the commons from where they could see a long stretch of road. Mathilde & Augustine stood by the window. A truck appeared. It wasn't going fast. It stopped for a moment in front of the abandoned sheepfold. "Continue," said Mathilde to Jean-François, "but be careful." The truck started again, then stopped in front of an empty barn. "Continue," said Mathilde. The truck was advancing slowly. Jean-François tapped quickly. The truck skirted the farmland. "Another second & I'll be done with one telegram," said Jean-François. "Go ahead," Mathilde said. The truck was approaching. "Run off with the transmitter into the woods," said Mathilde. Jean-François hesitated — he wouldn't leave the two women alone. Gestapo agents exited the truck. "It's an order," said Mathilde. When the German police entered the farm, they found two women in black quietly knitting. After a purely routine search they apologized.

———

Augustine's 17 year-old daughter joined us. She wanted to long ago. She took advantage of Mathilde's visit & authority to force her mother's consent. Madeleine will be coupled as a liaison agent with Félix's wife, who is doing very good work.

———————

When we ask people who, without belonging to an organization, help us hide weapons or take in comrades, when we ask them what could please them, they often say: "Have the B.B.C. say something for us." It seems to them a wonderful reward.

———————

We had a very safe relay in V. An old petrol station — closed since the armistice — that was overseen by an exceptionally loyal and discrete little old man with teary eyes. We had to take advantage of his services. Absolute prudence is impossible. There are so many losses that we are forced to overburden those who remain at large.

Two Gestapo agents showed up for the old man. He received them very politely and, when they permitted him to lower his arms, he took a revolver from under a pile of rags and shot them. Then he went out and called the driver of the German car for help. As the other rushed toward him, he put a bullet through his neck then fled in the Gestapo's car.

Madeleine & Félix's widow have been arrested. Denounced by a militiaman. Mathilde decided he must die.

One of our intelligence agents encountered a patrol of four German soldiers in an absolutely forbidden zone. He fired quickly & precisely. He killed all of them and then committed suicide. He could have escaped. The path was clear. We knew from the testimony of two Germans who survived and who were handed over to us. But our friend was too afraid of being caught, tortured, and speaking. He had always intended the last bullet for himself. He obeyed automatically.

The fear of not enduring interrogation torments and of revealing names and meeting places is for many an almost pathological obsession. Our people dread less suffering and tortures than their own potential weakness. Nobody knows what he is capable of enduring. And one trembles at the thought of having to live — even for a short time — with the feeling of having sent comrades to death, ruining a network, destroying work to which they'd been more attached than life. For some, this apprehension reaches a point of obsession. They cannot sleep; they cannot wake up without it dominating their minds. They check their doses of poison a hundred times a day. And they kill themselves before having exhausted their chances. Because to survive is at the same time to risk speaking.

Mathilde and the Bison have executed the militiaman who had denounced Félix's wife & young Madeleine.

My photograph had been provided by care of the Gestapo to every *commissariat*, to every prefecture, to every train station, to the gendarmeries, to the various services of the *Sûreté*. I found out through a police officer that is on our side. He advises me to stay with him. It's the safest shelter for the moment.

This policeman, who vowed that he was on our side, came into the resistance by a kind of shock, a revelation. About ten months later he was picked out, along with other French police officers, to assist with one of the Gestapo's operations. Two cars brought the German & French agents to the C.P. of a network that housed a transmitter, an arms depot, and a dozen people. The Gestapo agents directed the search. The Frenchman obeyed without saying a word. The police officer that is hiding me today wanted to open a sack that a young woman was carrying. She threw it in his face shouting: "Kraut, dirty kraut." The young woman had a beautiful face, delicate & fragile, but fearless. "I'm not a kraut," Leroux said despite himself.

— Then it's worse, said the young woman.

— I felt like I was going to pieces inside, Leroux told me, & my eyes clouded with tears.

It's then that he *saw* what was going on around him. They put handcuffs on an officer from the other war and whose lapel had the most glorious ribbons. The radio operator, a teenager, had his face smashed in with truncheons because he had swallowed some papers. They were twisting the wrists of a young girl to extract a confession.

Leroux made nothing more than robotic movements during the search and when it was finished he wandered through the city as if disembodied. A friend accompanied him, another officer who had also helped the Gestapo. This friend prevented him from killing himself.

— I would've done it, Leroux told me; I would've surely done it. When I remembered that two years ago I gave a hand to it without thinking, out of routine, when I thought again of all the good people, all the big-hearted women that I ratted on, arrested, handed over to the krauts, it seemed that I had leprosy ... That's what I've suffered!

He exclaimed all this to his friend. The other understood, too. He said to Leroux: "It's no use destroying yourself. We can try to make up for it."

They each contacted a different organization through the intermediary of prisoners. They immediately gave such assurances to the resistance and took such risks that they were accepted. Leroux's friend, after a magnificent job, had been burned. He had to go to England with some resistance leaders with whom he escaped. Leroux continues to serve on our behalf.

———————

One thought doesn't let Leroux rest. It's that there are French police whose relentlessness is equal to that of the Germans.

— I'm forced to forgive, said Leroux, the inspectors who do their job as I did, by decree, without revolt, but without zeal. They obey Vichy, they obey the Marshal. They haven't learned to think. But the others, those who are zealous, those who work overtime, with full heart against the patriots. Those, goddammit … *Those* …

And Leroux tells me of a chief inspector in Lyon who had sharpened the tip of a shovel with razor wire to put above barefoot captives who didn't want to talk. And Leroux tells me about the Paris "terrorist" brigade assigned to hunt down communists and whose agents are proud of having a greater imagination for torture than the Gestapo.

There is in Leroux more than a simple reaction of patriotism and of basic humanity against those people. There is the shame and anger that they are in the same profession as him.

Yesterday he brought me a copy of a clandestine newspaper of the *francs-tireurs* and partisans, *France d'abord*, seized by the police, and he read me the following note:

— "At Beuvry, Pas-de-Calais, the Police Commissaire & several subordinates had arrested and tortured numerous compatriots and boasted of shooting the F.T.P. on the spot.

A punishment was necessary.

On March 23, the mayor of Beuvry, a friend of Commissaire Théry, was forced to drive his car with a small group of the F.T.P. and to bring them to the commissariat. The agents who wanted to resist were pulled from combat. But the secretary succeeded in escaping. It was therefore not necessary to telephone the *commissaire* to contact him. In effect, after half an hour, two columns of agents and gendarmes flushed the houses of the *commissaire* before which the F.T.P. had taken a fighting position. Both sides opened fire. The *commissaire* succeeded in wounding a patriot. At that moment, the machine-gunner of the group blasted the *commissaire*, then another flurry of bullets followed against Sirven, the gendarmerie sergeant-major who murdered a patriot last year.

Their leaders killed, some fifteen policemen & gendarmes, taken to panic, fled. The small group of F.T.P. withdrew, carrying nine revolvers & interesting papers found at the commissariat.

Policemen sold to the krauts who arrest and torture patriots should know that the example of Beuvry will be followed."

I don't think that a *franc-tireur* or partisan could have read this report with as much joy and with such a feeling of sated vengeance as police inspector Leroux.

Another torment for Leroux is that he cannot help all the comrades of the resistance with whom his duties bring him into contact. Young Gaullist girls mixed in with the most obscene prostitutes, thieves, murderers; magnificent patriots;

elite officers mixed with convicts & treated like them; boys who have been courageous and strong and who are reduced by hunger and fever to the state of wrecks, who go crazy in cells ... People who by mere request of the Germans are deported, tortured, shot. And all regard Leroux with suspicion, with disgust. But he must wait for our orders and can only help one out of a hundred prisoners escape. And he must all the same justify himself in his job, be it ever so little. He is attached to the Gestapo. We need him to remain in that position.

———

Sometimes there is some compensation for Leroux. For instance, he just listened for two hours to a German lecture on how to detect and prevent parachute drops. Yet, he will receive parachutists tonight. A police car will bring back the British goods.

———

Félix's widow and little Madeleine were taken to room 87. They stripped them completely. A man and a woman of the Gestapo (a married couple, it is believed) interrogated them while sticking red-hot pins in their stomachs & under their nails. Félix's widow and Madeleine also underwent the dental drill that penetrates to the jawbone. They revealed nothing. Between each ordeal they sang the *Marseillaise*. This scene, which seems as if taken out of an absurd melodrama in the worst possible taste, is recorded in an official German report. Leroux had sent me a copy. He also made known to me that the two women vowed that they would not talk.

———————

This story has ravaged Mathilde. Her face was literally blackened. She keeps repeating endlessly: "If I don't get Madeleine out of there, God will never forgive me." The thought that she persuaded Augustine to let her daughter go into the resistance eviscerates Mathilde. She doesn't think of Félix's widow. It's the image of the girl that haunts her. She is the same age as Mathilde's eldest, whose gentle, common features I saw in a photograph.

———————

One of my friends has left for London. The Germans came to his house during his absence. They took his son, who is 11, on the pretext that he had made Gaullist propaganda at his school. They put the child against a white wall with a very powerful projector shooting into his eyes, and they interrogated him all night about his father's whereabouts. The child repeated the same story all night. His father was involved with a woman other than his mother and because of it his parents fought. His mother had sent his father packing. "Because of those quarrels I'm not well educated and I speak badly at school," said the little boy against the white wall.

Mathilde did something crazy. She tried to remove Madeleine with great force right in the street when she came out of prison only to be driven back to room 87. Mathilde had the Bison, Jean-François, and three men from the combat groups with her. They are all fanatics like Mathilde. They almost succeed, but a charge of S.S. disrupted them. They fell back. A chase through the streets. Our people went to the rooftops. District identified. Shooting from the chimneys. Many Germans gunned down, but they got two of our people. Another wounded taken. Mathilde and Jean-François succeeded in escaping. Mathilde has aggravated little Madeleine's situation, & for a mere liaison agent has demolished an entire combat section.

Leroux showed me an underground newspaper that I didn't know of. It's a hostage newspaper. It's called *Le Patriote du Camp de V*, a small handwritten journal. It was published four times. Each of the four issues is in a different handwriting. They killed a lot at Camp de V.

There are two poems in one of those issues, written by a boy of 19, a worker. In between he was sentenced to death.

Here's the first:

> *Farewell C, my old friend,*
> *At seventeen, in complete drunkenness,*
> *And without mercy for your youth,*
> *They killed you, those murderers.*
>
> *Without fear of the comrade,*
> *You fell with valiance.*
> *And the cry of "Vive le France!"*
> *Was your last, my comrade.*
>
> *Your beautiful smile is gone.*
> *And we who remain in prison*
> *For revenge we emerge.*
> *Goodbye, my old friend!*

And here's the second:

> *We are all communists*
> *And for having a loud scream*
> *We are on the dismal list*
> *Of those who go to the stake.*
>
> *Oh! you who are free,*
> *Oh! you our fighting brothers,*
> *We are always by your side,*
> *Not one of us will falter.*

For us the hour of death advances,
It already reaches out,
But we will have vengeance,
That task will be yours.

———————

Extract from the report of a group leader of *Francs-Tireurs and Partisans*:

"A train that left the town of X every evening loaded with krauts on leave was reported to us. After several reconnaissances, the moment to act had come. My seven men united in Bois-Mesnil at eight in the evening.

After the instructions had been dispatched, we advanced two by two, behind our scouts. On reaching the tracks, all was quiet, and we set up a machine gun on a hill overlooking the embankment & let the patrol go by.

Then I set up two remote lookouts, connected to us by means of a string hanging from the ballast, to silently warn us in case of danger. Nine o'clock! With three men I began to "unbolt" one of the rails from the track (our wrenches were carefully wound in rags this time) while leaving four other bolts in place so that the passenger train could still get through. We lay down as soon as it was in sight. Then in the six minutes remaining before the passage of the kraut train, we removed the last bolts, dragging the track to the side and driving three iron bolts in the holes so as to keep it out of alignment. We finished just in time to take up our position on the embankment opposite the sabotage point.

At 9:35 P.M., the kraut train, going at a good speed, derailed as expected. We held a rapid & sustained fire of all of our weapons on the krauts exiting from the least demolished cars and we quickly retreated following the planned route for each pair.

We didn't meet anyone and the railway guards heard nothing of our work.

There must've been sixty killed and hundreds wounded. All the men had been outstanding *but but registration number 7308 had been the object of a reprimand for having lit a cigarette while waiting for the passenger train."*

The heads of all the interlinked organizations have decided to meet. The boss has asked me to come. Leroux begs me not to make this long journey. He says that my description is everywhere & I'm at the top of the list of wanted people. That was inevitable. I'm the oldest of the surviving comrades.

To lead the Gestapo to the location of a transmitting post that has never existed, the Bison had himself driven at night on a route that we had established in advance. A chain was stretched between two trees across a narrow road. The "passive defense" headlights had not been caught in time. The car gave against the chain at full speed. Mathilde and Jean-François wiped the Germans clean with tommy guns. The Bison has a broken arm but he will recover.

I went to the resistance meeting. Leroux accompanied me with a warrant. I was his prisoner. Ideal safe conduct.

In three stations we met with convoys of deportation deserters. Those young men had handcuffs, leg irons, shaved heads. Some waved their chained hands & shouted: "Volunteers …! Volunteers …!" Others sang the *Marseillaise*, punctuating the song with the noise of their rattling shackles.

The meeting lasted a long time. When it was concluded the boss said:

— There are fourteen of us here. In coming each of us took a fatal risk. I'm not sure that the practical results warrant it. No importance. Underground France has held a council in defiance of terror. It was worth it.

And Saint Luc (I like to call him by the name given to him by his brother), Saint Luc said to me again:

— We're only fourteen, but how different! Look at M and his inspired, furrowed, and somewhat secret face like the face of a Da Vinci. Look at B's violent neck and his impassioned eyes. Look at the obstinate way in which J sucks at his pipe. Look at R's hard, terrible hands. Look at how A timidly wipes his pince-nez. You've heard them speak. For some the sole object is the war against the German. Others are already considering issues of class and post-war politics. And others are already thinking of Europe & dreams of world brotherhood. But everything's been discussed with friendliness. It was worth the trouble.

And Saint Luc added:

— We're only fourteen, but we're borne up by thousands and probably millions of men. To protect ourselves, combat groups guard all the access points that lead to this retreat. And will die before letting anyone get to us. However, no one here has pride or even a sense of power. We know that our soldiers change their names a hundred times and that they have neither shelter nor faces. They go in secret in shapeless shoes on sunless roads void of glory. We know that our army is famished and pure. It is an army of shadows. The miraculous army of love & misfortune. And I've become conscious here that we're only the shadows of those shadows and the reflection of that love and that misfortune. That, above all, Gerbier, was worth the trouble.

———————

Back at Leroux's. I transmit the warning to newcomers who wish to enter the organization that they must not count on more than three months of freedom, that is to say, of life. This will prevent nothing undoubtedly, but it is more honest.

6

A VIGIL IN THE HILTERIAN AGE

The German soldier stopped pacing the corridor and pressed his helmeted face against the wicket. Among those sentenced to death, Gerbier alone noticed this amalgam of metal, flesh, and scrutinizing eyes that had blocked the opening of the wicket. He was the only one not convinced that life was finished. He didn't feel himself to be in a death state.

The German soldier's eyes crossed those of Gerbier.

— He doesn't seem to be afraid, thought the soldier.

The other convicts were sitting around on bare slabs and talking in low tones.

"Neither do they, thought the soldier. Yet this is the morning."

The soldier wondered for a moment how he would've behaved if he'd known that he had only two hours to live. He wondered also what these men could have done. Then he yawned. The watch was long. It was better to pace the hallway till the execution. This was war, after all.

Gerbier glanced back at his comrades who were chained at the feet like him. The rooms of the former French barracks had livid grey walls. The feeble electric light gave the same tint to the condemned.

There were six of them besides Gerbier. The one who was speaking at the moment when Gerbier began to listen distractedly to their words had a pronounced Breton accent. His extreme youth was perceptible only in his still naive intonations. But his face, simple in line and so rough it seemed carved in boxwood, showed no trace of it. It was frozen in a kind of heavy disbelief. The protruding eyes still bore the expression of a man who has been wounded by images he can no longer erase.

— This is the second time that I'm to be shot, said the kid. The first wasn't real because I was only fifteen then. It was in Brest and on account of some machine guns that French soldiers leaving for England must have abandoned. We didn't want them to go to the krauts. We buried them. A postman betrayed us. He got a knife in the shoulders, but twelve guys a bit older than me were executed. Given my age, they'd changed the judgment at the last minute and I was sent to Germany as a civilian prisoner. I never knew how long my sentence was. We lived, we died, without knowing anything. During the thirty months that passed before my escaping, I hadn't received one package, not one letter. At home they had no idea what'd become of me. My mother, she remained disturbed in the head.

"In those civilian prisons, they had all kinds: Austrians, Poles, Czechs, Serbs, & then naturally many Germans. We were hungry ... we were hungry! ... To suppress their appetites, the guys smoked bits of straw they'd pulled out of their beds and rolled in strips of newspaper. I had never smoked. I was forced to start ... I was so hungry!"

Gerbier handed his companions a half-full pack of cigarettes. Each took one and lit his except the oldest, a farmer with grey hair as hard as boar bristles. He put his cigarette behind his ear & said: "I'll keep it for later on." They knew he meant execution time. The German soldier smelt the odor of tobacco in the hallway but said nothing. It was he who had sold Gerbier his pack of cigarettes.

— When we were caught smoking that straw we were punished with twenty-five stick blows, said the young Breton with bulging eyes. But since we were punished for anything, for everything, we thought, a little more, a little less ... and we smoked anyway.

"The other prisoners were forced to administer the beatings. They stripped you bare and struck you. The guards counted the blows. If the guys weren't going at it hard enough, the guards would take their turn. As for the death sentences — and there were plenty ... it was all the time ... it was the same system. They chose buddies, the best friends of the condemned, to do the hangings. But he wasn't strung up as soon as he was condemned. In between, days and often weeks would pass ... We knew nothing, I tell you. The gallows were there, in the yard, ready ... The convicts — they painted a large black cross on their backs & knees —, they went on working ... And then one fine morning, we were lined up in a square around the gallows & four friends were made the executioners of some unfortunate guy. The other convicts with their black crosses, they waited for their day without knowing which it would be. You have to have seen their eyes to understand ...

"Once, it was a Pole who was to be hanged. His four friends, also Polish, before noosing him up, began to kneel before him to ask for forgiveness. He made the sign of the cross over each of them and they embraced one another. You have to have seen it to understand ...

"They threw the bodies in a mass grave and we put quick-lime over them. It was always us who did it. There weren't only the condemned to bury ... There were those who died of hunger, of disease. And there were those who could no longer live in that way. Those guys, they walked up to a guard. The guard exhorted them. If they didn't stop, the guard fired."

The young Breton with the boxwood face sniffled. He had no handkerchief.

— But the most terrible thing in my mind isn't the dead, he said. It's the evening that they made me change cells and they put me in with a poor old man whose hair and beard were entirely white. This old man, on seeing me, he scuttled into a corner and thrust his hands before his face as if I was going to hit him. I first thought he was crazy ... There were a lot of madmen ... But no, he had good reason. Only he was a Jew. And so, the Germans ... the German prisoners, I mean to say (because I don't mean to speak of the guards), they beat him, they dragged him by the beard around the cell, they banged his old white head against the walls. Prisoners against another prisoner ... Against a poor old man ...

The man next to Gerbier gave a nervous start. He was small, dark, with darting, melancholic eyes.

"A Jew," thought Gerbier.

He didn't know his companions. They had been together since the last vigil only.

— So, when I escaped and when, after a few months, they wanted to send me to work in Germany, I defended myself with a knife, said the kid without changing his expression. He was eighteen years old. And here I am … This time, it's real … I'm old enough …

The farmer with the cigarette on his ear asked:

— You've bled many of them, son?

— I haven't had time, said the Breton.

— Well, I've done my share, said the farmer.

His lips, covered with hard, grey hairs, curled up. He wasn't laughing. He didn't smile. It was more like the movements of a hunting dog's flews expressing contentment. The farmer's teeth were black and solid.

— If I went to confession, he said, I'd have to admit I didn't think up the idea entirely on my own. Chance has been a good friend.

The farmer blinked & rubbed his hands as if speaking of an advantageous market.

— My property is located along a highway. The Fritzes had their quarters nearby. They always came to my place to ask me if I had anything to drink. I sold it to them, and expensive … Always so much to the good … They only came one by one because it was forbidden and they were always wary of their comrades. And then, one evening, there was a half-drunk NCO who didn't see the trapdoor to the cellar & he fell in. It's deep, my cellar … The Fritz had broken his neck good & well. I went down, I found him dead. I didn't want anything to do with this story so I buried him right then and there … It may well have been that corpse which set me to thinking … I can't be too sure, but, then, a few days later, the trapdoor was still open when a fritz came in. He also drank a glass too much and he fell in as well … Only, with that accident, I helped him a bit. And I buried him next to the first … And then, there was another … and another … I took count. It went up to nineteen … In the end, I was going too fast … I couldn't resist … It transfixed me, that trapdoor. A fritz disappearing every month, it can pass muster. But two or three a week, you must admit, it's difficult to accept. The *Kommandantur* started investigating. They ended up checking my cellar. And the bottom of my cellar, well, it climbed too high, the bottom … There were three layers of fritzes. So, I'm here … I've done my share."

The farmer's lips again made a movement that recalled the expression of a satisfied hunting dog.

Gerbier thought: "We ought to take him into our combat groups." And he thought almost simultaneously: "But he will be shot in a few minutes." And about the same time an inner voice said within Gerbier, "And so am I …" But he didn't recognize this voice. It wasn't his. And he couldn't believe it.

Meanwhile, a third condemned man was already speaking. Gerbier understood that each of them listened to his companions with indifference & only out of courtesy. Each had only one desire, one eagerness — to deliver the essence of his being before dying.

— I've done my part too, though I'm not yet twenty, said the condemned man who had taken his turn to speak.

In him his youth burst forth in the fire of his voice, in the life of his face, and up until the little brown and tender mustache that he had grown in prison. With his bulging forehead & strong shoulders, he looked like a steer.

— I'm a Lorrain, from annexed Lorraine. I was studying at the university when the krauts had announced that my class would be mobilized six months later in the German army. I didn't hesitate for a second, you can imagine. I had time to spend Christmas with my family and get away. It was a beautiful Christmas Eve. I don't know how my mother was able to get hold of a goose. My father had taken out the last good bottles. I was in a bit of a funk about leaving without warning. At the end of the meal my father hugged & kissed me all the way to the door. He opened it. And he said: "We know your duty." My mother gave me a suitcase she had prepared, and some money. In the morning, I crossed the French border. At that point I thought, "Old man, with such parents, you won't be able to lead a quiet little life and wait for a victory to be won for you." In Paris, I tried to make myself useful. I knew a group with great young people. I worked for a freethinking newspaper. I must tell you that I wanted to be a writer. Eh, well, I could be … and in a historical period such as there has never been. In one hundred years, a thousand years, we'll reread these papers, you'll see …"

Gerbier considered for a moment those cheeks colored with such vivid blood that it was stronger than the wretched light and the livid grey reflections of the walls.

"That boy's got temperament," thought Gerbier. "He must have written for *L'Étudiant Patriote* or *Les Lettres Françaises*."

Another condemned man spoke. A man of very slender build and very delicate features. Although he was sitting Turkish style, his torso was perfectly straight, like a cuirass. His eyes were luminous & his voice one of singular clarity.

— It's not a deliberate action that brought me amongst you, gentlemen, he said. Despite the feelings that I happened to have, I didn't dare take sides against the Marshal. I wasn't quite sure of my intelligence. My confessor — and I've always followed his advice — suggested that I wait until I had greater self-clarity. I had a small castle and some land. I had four children. I lived for them. No, I've done nothing, but I couldn't refuse asylum to the persecuted. I took in Englishmen and escaped prisoners, fleeing patriots, & Jewish children.

The man beside Gerbier nervously shook his head.

— They finally arrested me. During the investigation I was able to see my family. My children, in the beginning, didn't recognize me. I was dirty. I had a week-old beard and I was already dressed like a robber. When I kissed them, they were afraid. With their eyes they demanded relief from their mother. Finally, the eldest, who was seven, and who went to a little girls' school, asked me: "Papa, it's not true that you've acted very badly against the Marshal, is it?" For the first time in my life, I didn't know how to respond to that child. In class they did everything to make them love the Marshal. And the Marshal kept me behind bars for two years in the former un-occupied zone, and when the Germans occupied it, the Marshal handed me over to them. I've forgiven all my enemies. It's in regard to the Marshal that I've had the greatest difficulty in showing myself a Christian."

The man with the lively, melancholic eyes seated beside Gerbier began to speak in such a hurry that the words seemed to cluster together. Gerbier wondered if it was due to racial impatience or simply because time was pressing.

— I am a rabbi, said the man beside Gerbier, a rabbi of a big city. Because of this, the Germans assigned me to the committee charged with identifying the Israelites who would not declare themselves. You follow me? ... There are five people in this kind of committee: two Germans, two French-Catholics, and one French Israelite. I was the last. You follow me? ... Every week they brought men and women before us whom the occupation authorities suspected of being Israelites, and we had to say whether they were or not. An Israelite, and especially a rabbi, is more likely than anyone else to recognize his people. You follow me? ... The Germans definitely thought so. And they had forewarned me. The first time that I would say no when they could prove that it was so, I would be shot. You follow me? ... Only, if I said yes, people were deported to Poland to die. Nice situation for a rabbi ...

The man beside Gerbier bowed his face toward the pavement with a distressed & almost guilty expression. He sighed:

I always said no ... So, here I am ...

The sixth condemned man kept holding one hand against the left side of his face. He was missing an eye and his flesh was as if scalded.

— I'm a communist, and an escaped prisoner also, he said. When I returned, I found neither my wife, nor my sister, nor their kids. Nobody knew anything. This is what happened: my sister, she's married to a party deputy. He was in prison. My sister began to collect *sous* whilst milling amongst the comrades in order to send him packages. One day she learned that the wife of another deputy was arrested for this crime. My sister never had very strong nerves. She lost her head. And as she was living together with my wife, panic seized her also. So they left to hide away somewhere. But they had no place to go. They were afraid of everybody. And they didn't want to get anyone in trouble. They finally found an abandoned shack in the fields. They left only during the night to look for potatoes, which they dug up. Then they ate roots. They lived for months without bread, without fire, without towels, without soap. And also the kids. Two from me, one from my sister. When I finally got a hold of them they were a fine sight to see, I swear to you ... Now they're living with our comrades.

The man suddenly clenched his teeth & growled:

— Goddamned eye ... How it makes me suffer ...

He took a deep breath & continued in a singularly flat voice:

— And me, they'll never know what became of me. The Gestapo was unable to identify me. I shall be shot under a false name.

The man instinctively turned toward Gerbier and the others followed suit. Gerbier had decided to remain silent. He felt that he was inwardly attuned to his companions. He had nothing to confide to them. And they had no curiosity about his confidences.

If they were questioning him with their eyes it was simple politeness. Yet Gerbier also spoke:

— I don't want to start running now, he said.

Nobody understood. Gerbier remembered that these condemned men were all isolated members of the resistance or strangers to the city.

— Here, said Gerbier, they fire away with machine guns and we're on the fly. I think they do it by way of training… Unless it's an amusement … They let you go, you take your momentum, you gain twenty, thirty meters. Then, fire … It's a good exercise for shooting at moving silhouettes. I won't give them that pleasure.

Gerbier took out his pack of cigarettes, split them in half, & distributed the remaining three.

— No one will want to run, said the student.

— It's no use, said the farmer.

— And it's really losing face, said the squire.

The amalgam of helmet, flesh, & scrutinizing eye filled the wicket. The German soldier shouted a few words to Gerbier:

— He asked that we hurry with our smoking, Gerbier translated. They're coming for us in a moment. He doesn't want to get into trouble.

— You take whatever troubles you can, that we know, said the communist, shrugging his shoulders.

The student had become very pale. The squire crossed himself. The rabbi began to mutter Hebraic verses.

— This time it's for real, said the 18 year-old Breton.

Gerbier gave a half-smile. The farmer slowly took the cigarette that he had behind his ear ...

7

THE SHOOTING RANGE

The central part of the old barracks was connected to the shooting range via a very long vaulted corridor. The seven condemned men entered it one by one, flanked by a formation of S.S. soldiers. Gerbier was at about the middle of the line. The student walked at the head and the farmer was the last in file. The condemned advanced slowly. They still had shackles on. The corridor had no opening to the outside. At regular intervals the crowned light bulbs cast a vague glow. The shadows of the condemned and those of their armed guards formed a giant convoy and flickered on the walls. In the resounding silence of the corridor, the booted tread of the soldiers made a deep, heavy sound and at the same time you could hear the rattling chains of the condemned and their creaking irons.

— It creates a kind of symphony, Gerbier said to himself. I wish the boss could hear it.

Gerbier remembered the expression that had come over Luc Jardie's face when he spoke about music. And Gerbier was as dazzled to encounter that face in the vaulted corridor.

The chains clanked. The irons creaked.

It's really curious, said Gerbier to himself. Our shackles remind me of the boss. Without them … maybe.

And suddenly, Gerbier thought:

"I'm an idiot."

He'd just realized that any image and any sensation would've brought him back to Luc Jardie by an unforeseen and inevitable detour.

"The word love has meaning for me only when it applies to the boss. He means more to me than anything," Gerbier said to himself. But it was then that an answer came to him from his guts: "More than anything & less than life."

The shadows danced, the shackles groaned.

Saint Luc is whom I love most in life, but Saint Luc could disappear and I would still like to live.

The shadows … the sound of the chains … Gerbier reflected faster and ever faster.

"And I'm going to die … and I'm not afraid … It's impossible not to be afraid when you'll die … It's because I'm too narrow-minded, too animal to believe it. But if I don't believe till the last moment, till the final limit, I will never die. What a discovery! And since it would please the boss, I must go deeper into it … I must …"

At this point Gerbier's scintillating meditation was suddenly ruptured. At the first moment, he didn't understand the cause of this interruption. Then he heard a song that filled the entire space of the corridor. Then he recognized this song: *La Marseillaise*. The student had begun it. The others had immediately taken it up. The student, the rabbi, and the farmer had beautiful, full, and passionate voices. It was they that Gerbier heard best. But he wouldn't listen. He wanted to think. Those voices interfered with him. And above all, he didn't want to sing.

"*La Marseillaise*... it's always done in such cases," Gerbier said to himself. For a moment he rediscovered his half-smile.

The file of the condemned advanced slowly. The song passed over Gerbier without engaging him.

"They don't want to think, and me, I want to ...," he said. And he waited with savage impatience till the familiar stanzas were exhausted. The corridor was long.

"I still have time for myself," thought Gerbier.

La Marseillaise came to an end.

"Quick, quick, I must explore my discovery," thought Gerbier. But the strong, pure voice of the student rose again. And this time Gerbier was seized and tightly held within as if by a magic hand. *Le Chant du Départ* had always affected him like that. Gerbier was sensitive to its accent, its words. He stiffened. He didn't want to do as the others. He had an essential problem to solve. Yet he felt the melody welling up in his chest. He gritted his teeth. His companions were singing...

Un Français doit vivre pour elle...
Pour elle un Français doit mourir...

Gerbier grit his teeth harder because he was already singing deep in his throat. Would he get carried away?

"I will not yield ... I will not yield ..." Gerbier said to himself. "It's the herd instinct ... I don't want to sing just as I don't want to run before the machine guns."

This link helped him to contain the song ready to escape from his body. He had the feeling of having vanquished an inner danger.

The shackled row finally reached a small door in the thickness of the wall on the left. The shadows stopped dancing. The creaking chains fell silent. And so did the song. A guard opened the door. A natural light shot across part of the corridor. The student reprised the *Marseillaise* & the condemned, one behind the other, penetrated into the enclosure of their death.

It was a classic military shooting range. A bare rectangle enclosed by rather high walls. Against the back wall and separated from it by a narrow space, you could see a mound for holding targets. Some old scraps of fabric and paper trembled on its slopes in the sharp morning breeze. The light was clear and sad. One by one the condemned stopped singing. They had just discerned, a few paces away, the machine guns. An S.S. lieutenant, very lean, with a metallic face, commanded the firing squad. He looked at his watch.

— Precision kraut, grumbled the communist worker.

The student breathed in the fresh air with all his strength and tugged on his mustache.

— I don't want to run ... I will not ... said Gerbier.

The others, as if entranced, never let their gaze shift away from the S.S. lieutenant. He shouted an order. The soldiers gave a turn of their keys & unlocked the shackles, which fell with a muffled thud to the floor. Gerbier trembled to suddenly feel himself so light. He had the impression that his legs were all new, very young — he had to try them out immediately. They demanded the field. They were going to carry him away at a winged speed. Gerbier looked at his companions. Their muscles were agitated by the same impatience. The student especially could barely control himself. Gerbier looked at the S.S. officer. He was tapping a cigarette on the nail of his right thumb. He had glaucous, frozen eyes.

"He knows very well what my legs want," thought Gerbier suddenly. "He's preparing for the show."

Gerbier felt more securely chained by the assurance of that man than he had been by the irons. The officer looked at his watch and addressed the condemned in very distinct French:

— In one minute you will put your backs to the machine guns and face the mound, he said. You will run as fast as you can. We will not fire immediately. We will give you a chance. Those who hide behind the mound will be executed later, with the next group of the condemned.

The officer spoke with a strong, mechanical voice, as if announcing a regulation maneuver. Having finished, he lit his cigarette.

— We can always try … We've nothing to lose … said the farmer to the rabbi.

The latter didn't reply, but his eyes avidly gauged the distance that separated him from the mound. Without knowing it, the student & the young Breton did the same.

The soldiers aligned the seven men as the officer commanded. And not seeing the weapons, feeling their muzzles on his back, Gerbier was seized with a strange contraction. A spring seemed to throw him forward.

— Go ... said the S.S. lieutenant.

The student, the rabbi, the young Breton, the farmer, they set off immediately. The communist, Gerbier, and the squire did not stir. But they had the impression of swinging back and forth as if they were struggling to maintain equilibrium between two opposing forces.

"I don't want ... I don't want to run ..." repeated Gerbier to himself.

From his revolver, the S.S. lieutenant fired three bullets — they sped alongside the cheeks of Gerbier and his companions. And the equilibrium was broken ... The three condemned men followed their comrades.

Gerbier had no sense of advancing of his own accord. The spring that he felt winding tightly within him unraveled and he hurtled right past everyone. He could still think. And he knew that this race that was bringing him in the direction of the mound served no purpose. No one ever came back alive from a shooting range. There were not even wounded. The machine-gunners knew their business.

The bullets buzzed over his head, against his flanks.

"Bullets for nothing," said Gerbier ... "Elite marksmen ... It's they that stress the pace ... Waiting for a more meritorious distance ... Grotesque to tire oneself." And yet, with each whistle, Gerbier lengthened his stride. His mind became confused. The body outweighed thought — soon he would only be a fear-stricken rabbit. He prohibits himself from watching the mound. He didn't want that hope. Watching the mound was watching death; he didn't feel himself in a state of death ... As long as one thinks, one cannot die. But the body was winning ... still winning over thought. Gerbier remembered how this body, against itself, had relaxed in London, at the Ritz Hotel ... The tips of the candles flickered before him ... The dinner at the old lady's with the boss. The tips of the candles blazing, blazing, like sharp suns.

And then darkness. A wave of thick black smoke spread from one end of the shooting range to the other, spanning its entire width. A shadowy curtain had fallen. Gerbier's ears buzzed so much that he didn't hear the explosions from the smoke grenades. But because his mind had not yet reached the breaking point he understood that this thickening fog was intended for him. And since he was the only one who had never accepted the death state, he was the only one to take advantage of the fog.

The other condemned ones stopped short. They had abandoned themselves to their muscles for an animal game. The game ended; their muscles no longer carried them. Gerbier, he gave his every breath, all his force. Now he no longer thought at all. The bursts of bullets followed him, surrounded him, but the gunners couldn't make more than guesswork. A bullet shred a piece of flesh from his arm. Another burned his thigh. He ran faster. He passed the mound. Behind was the wall. And on that wall, Gerbier saw ... *it was certain* ... a rope ...

Without using his feet, without feeling that he was pulling himself up by the strength of his wrists, like a gymnast, Gerbier reached the crest of the wall. A few hundred meters away he saw … *it was certain* … a car. He jumped … he stole away … The Bison was waiting, the engine running, the car began to roll. Mathilde *&* Jean-François were inside.

———

The Bison drove very well, very fast. Gerbier was talking, and so were Jean-François and Mathilde. Jean-François was saying that it wasn't difficult. He'd always been a good grenade lobber in the Corps Franc. The important thing was to time the action as accurately as Mathilde had done. And she said that it was easy with the information they'd received.

Gerbier listened, responded. But it was all superficial. Without value. One single question, a crucial question obsessed his mind:

"And if I had not run? …"

Jean-François asked:

— Something wrong? The comrades who were left behind?

— No, said Gerbier.

He wasn't thinking of his companions. He was thinking of the S.S. lieutenant's metallic face and his dead eyes when he was tapping his cigarette on his fingernail, and that he was sure of making Gerbier run just as the others, like a crazed rabbit.

— I'm disgusted with living, Gerbier suddenly said.

The car crossed a bridge, then a forest. But Gerbier still saw the face of the S.S. officer, the cigarette, the thumbnail. He wanted to groan.

Until then Gerbier was sure that he detested the Germans with a fullness so perfect that it could not be increased any further. And of course also to have exhausted all the sources of a hatred that he cherished. Yet, he suddenly felt himself devoured by a fury that he hadn't yet known and that succeeded and renewed every other. But slimy & unhealthy & ashamed of itself. The fury of humiliation …

"He has dirtied my hatred …" thought Gerbier with despair.

His torment must have encroached upon his features for Mathilde made a gesture of which she appeared incapable. She took one of Gerbier's hands & held it in hers a moment. Gerbier didn't seem to notice the gesture. But he was more grateful to Mathilde for this than for having saved his life.

8

MATHILDE'S DAUGHTER

I

The little house had been uninhabited for a long time. It was in no way indistinguishable from the houses that were squeezed together on the cheap subdivision. It was only more humid than the others because its narrow garden was joined behind by marshland. It was on this side that Gerbier arrived with the Bison on the night following the adventure of the shooting range. Gerbier carried a suitcase containing records and documents. The Bison had a sack of grub. When the two men quietly entered the house, they were struck by the scent of mold.

— Nothing beautiful about safety, said the Bison.

He put his sack in the kitchen and went off. Gerbier carefully closed the door that led from the garden to the moldy little house.

He hadn't been out for three months.

The shutters had remained closed. The front door that led to the road had never been opened. Gerbier had never lit the fire (luckily spring had come very early). He had never used the electric light, not to increase the numbers on the meter. He worked by the light of a carefully shaded carbide lamp. He ate cold food. Once a week, with the mail, they brought him bread and preserves as good as could be found on the black market. The dates and times of those visits were scheduled in advance. Outside of them, Gerbier had no communication with the exterior world to hope for. The boss had ordered the most extreme prudence. Pictures of Gerbier were published and posted everywhere. The Gestapo had promised a huge bounty to informers.

When the nights were very dark, Gerbier would go into the garden. But he remained there only a few moments. A dog would bark, a door would slam in a neighboring house. Gerbier went back inside.

He had spent three months without allowing a spark of life to filter through.

II

Midnight approaching, Gerbier went barefoot from one to the other of the two rooms that made up the house. The carbide lamp lit just one part of the table on which rested papers: plans, messages, notes. Mail was ready. Gerbier no longer knew what to do. He paced for some time again. Then he shrugged his shoulders, grabbed a pack of cards, and began to play solitaire.

A key softly turned in the lock of the door leading on to the garden. Gerbier stopped playing solitaire but left the cards in place so as to later resume the game. He closed his eyes.

"The Bison, or Jean-François?" he asked himself. "If it's the Bison, the news of Mathilde will be ..." Gerbier's dry and hard lips contracted, and he furrowed his brow like one fighting against mental anguish.

— I'm becoming a superstitious idiot, Gerbier murmured.

The door to the hall was pushed open noiselessly and a silhouette was outlined on the threshold. Although there was a very dense shadow, Gerbier saw at once that this silhouette was not that of Jean-François or the Bison. The man was not their size. He had long hair & his back was slightly stooped. Gerbier got up but did not dare advance. The man laughed a naive, tender, almost silent laugh.

— It's ... it's you, boss, Gerbier whispered incredulously.

Jardie approached the table & each step seemed to define his face. Gerbier put his hands on Jardie's shoulders & gazed at him without blinking.

— I wanted to talk with you a little, said Jardie. Little brother Jean showed me the way. He's keeping watch outside.

Gerbier continued to hold Jardie by the shoulders & his fingers caressed the worn fabric of the jacket.

"The jaws and eyes are still firm," thought Jardie. "But he's no longer capable of his half-smile."

Gerbier finally said:

— The last place I saw you, boss, it was in the shooting range. I saw you among the candles. You remember, dinner

with candles when we were in London? I was on the run ...
because I ran like the others, you know ... I didn't want to
sing as they did because I'd found a solution to death & I was
thinking of you. I didn't sing, but I ran ... It's lamentable ...

— I don't think it's lamentable to be a man, Jardie said,
laughing.

Gerbier didn't seem to hear. He let his arms drop and said:

— During the interrogation I was handling myself well,
however. It's true that I wasn't too badly handled. I believe
they sense material that isn't too vulnerable. Unless there's a
mark that some people have. Some who use the most extensive precautions are taken. And others, such as the Bison or
your brother, they always escape ... They've the mark.

Jardie turned his gaze toward the cards spread out on the
table.

— I know ... I know, said Gerbier.

He rubbed his forehead again and suddenly shuffled the
cards.

— Sometimes I think that the prison was less stifling, he
said. There were my answers to calculate. I was looking for
a means of escape. I listened to others. I spoke with guards.
Here it's like a padded room. A wet, dark padding. Images
and thoughts go round in circles. There's the obsession of losing contact. I remember a communist in prison. Not the one
from the shooting range. Another. He'd been in hiding as long
as I was. A comrade, the only one he saw, was taken. No contact for weeks. It was worse than anything, he said. I know
that our partitioning is not as rigorous. I thought a great deal
about the discipline of the communists ...

— Gerbier, I'd like to know one thing, Jardie asked in a friendly tone. Is it loneliness that makes you talk so much and so quickly? Or do you do it to avoid thinking of Mathilde? …

III

Jean-François was crouching, invisible & motionless, against the wall of the house. Inside, his brother was performing a task unknown to him. His brother …

"What's the matter? Why isn't it the same anymore?" Jean-François wondered. "Who has changed? Him? Me? …"

Jean-François thought of his hunted, imprisoned, disfigured, strangled, shot companions. And also of the magnificent successes, the sabotages, the raids, the newspapers distributed by the thousands, the links with London, the parachute drops, the departures, the miracles of the underground tribe to which he belonged, martyred and victorious. Everything had its source & everything continued to be ordained in the little mansion on Rue de la Muette, with its harpsichord, its old servant, and the brother whom Jean-François had always known: he was defenseless, touching, and a little comical. For Jean-François he could not be the boss. But he could no longer be Saint Luc.

Jean-François didn't know what name to give to the man he had just led to the house.

IV

— We must talk about Mathilde tonight, said Jardie.

Gerbier threw his head back, as if he was altogether too close to Jardie and to the narrow circle of light that came from the shaded lamp.

— We have to, Jardie repeated softly.

— What for? Gerbier asked in a curt, almost hostile voice. There's nothing to say for the moment. I await news. Mail should arrive soon enough.

Jardie sat near the lamp. Gerbier likewise, but beyond its span of illumination. Unknowingly, he was dog-earing the corner of one of the cards he had shuffled. Then he went for a cigarette, but he had no more. He always exhausted his supply of tobacco before the mail returned.

— The news will be welcome, said Jardie. But I want to review the data of the problem with you as we once did with less human questions. You remember?

Gerbier remembered … Jardie's book … The little mansion on Rue de la Muette … Shared meditations. The lessons of knowledge, of wisdom …

Under the muffled lamp, in the musty room, Jardie's face was the same as it had been then. That ever so youthful smile and those white tufts. The line of the forehead. The pensive, chimerical eyes.

— Whatever you say, boss, said Gerbier. He felt again very free-spirited & capable of considering everything with serenity.

— Talk first, said Jardie.

— The facts connect as follows, said Gerbier. Mathilde was taken on May 27. They didn't harm her. She found a way to let us know very fast. And also that she was closely guarded. Then we learned that the Germans were investigating her past. The Gestapo easily found the anthropometric card made after her first arrest. The Germans know Mathilde's real name and her family's address. They descended on the Porte d'Orléans building. The Gestapo took the eldest daughter.

Jardie tilted his head a bit and wrapped his fingers round a small white tuft of hair that was near his temple and curled it. Not finding his gaze, Gerbier stopped talking. Jardie looked up but continued to play with his hair.

— There was also a photograph, he said.

— Yes, said Gerbier. That's the only mistake that Mathilde made against her safety. She kept a picture of her children on her. She thought she had found a way to conceal it. Till the ferrets of the Gestapo found it. The Germans felt right away that this was the breaking point in this nerveless woman. Especially since Mathilde, the Mathilde that we know, began to beg to be left her photograph. It's incredible…

— It's wonderful, said Jardie.

Then he asked:

— Have you seen the photograph?

— Mathilde showed it to me once, said Gerbier. Some insignificant children and a young girl without much expression, but fresh, gentle, proper.

Gerbier stopped again.

— So? Jardie asked.

— We received an S.O.S. from Mathilde, Gerbier said in a lower voice. The Germans gave her a choice: Either she would give up all the important people she knew among us, or her daughter would be sent to Poland to a brothel for soldiers returning from the Russian front.

Gerbier again looked in vain for a cigarette. Jardie stopped playing with his hair, put his hands flat on his knees, & said:

— This is the data of the problem. I've come in search of the solution.

Gerbier dog-eared the corner of a card and then another. He said:

— Mathilde may escape.

Jardie shook his head.

— You know something? Gerbier asked.

— I know nothing except that she *cannot* escape, and neither can she kill herself. The Gestapo isn't worried. The girl is responsible for everything.

— Mathilde can gain time, said Gerbier without looking at Jardie.

— How much? the latter asked.

Gerbier didn't answer. He had a terrible urge to smoke.

— The mail will never arrive tonight, he said furiously.

— Are you eager for news of Mathilde or for a cigarette? Jardie asked kindly.

Gerbier abruptly stood up and exclaimed:

— When I think of this woman, of what she was, of what she has done, and of what she has been reduced to … I can't think anymore … I … Oh! the bastards, the bastards …

— Not so loud, Gerbier, said Jardie, the house is uninhabited.

He took Gerbier gently by the wrist and made him sit down again.

V

Jean-François felt rather than saw or heard the Bison approach.

— Guillaume, Jean-François whispered, do not enter immediately, wait for a signal.

The Bison came and leaned against the wall near Jean-François.

— How are you? the young man whispered in his ear.

— So-so, said the Bison.

VI

Gerbier had rested both elbows on the table and his chin in the hollow of his clasped hands. It seemed to imprison the fury that stopped his throat and locked his lower jaw. He gazed fixedly, lengthily, at Jardie's lighted face. He asked:

— How, but how do you not tremble with hatred for those bastards? Is it not true that when you hear a story like that of Mathilde's daughter, you have an immediate desire to exterminate that whole people, to trample them, to ...

— No, Gerbier, not really, said Jardie. Think a little bit. A new episode, however frightful, surely isn't going to influence the overall feeling we can have for people. Something more or less cannot change a metaphysical conception. Everything that we have undertaken has been done so as to remain men of free thought. Hatred is a hindrance to free thought. I do not accept hatred.

Jardie began to laugh and it seemed as if his face and not the lamp had become the luminous focus of the room.

— I'm in the midst of a trick, said Jardie. What I just told you is a mental construct. And a mental construct is always made to justify an organic feeling. The truth is that I like people, simply that. And if I've got myself mixed up in all these stories, it's only against the inhuman part that exists in some of them.

Jardie laughed again.

— You know, it sometimes happens, he said, that I feel the urge to kill when I hear of Mozart or Beethoven being massacred! Is that hatred?

He wrapped a white tuft round a finger.

— I remember a fright that I'd had on the metro, said Jardie pensively. A man came and sat next to me, with a little goatee, a deformed shoulder, and dark glasses. He started looking at me through his glasses with an insistence and a strange expression. The police had never worried me. You were the only one to know both my real activity and my true identity. But still I was afraid. You never know. From time to time I raised my head & I always encountered that look. And then, once, the man winked at me. And I recognized Thomas, my dear Thomas, you know, the physicist, my teacher from the Sorbonne who was later executed. Yes, Thomas himself, who I had not seen since the war and who was beautifully made up. I was moved to embrace him, but he raised a finger and I understood that I mustn't recognize him. So we remained face to face looking at one another. From time to time he blinked at me from behind his dark glasses. Then he exited at a station. And I never saw him again.

Jardie let his hands fall to his knees & closed his eyelids halfway.

— That is the first wink that has remained in my memory, he continued. The wink that reestablished everything between two men. I've often dreamt that, some day, I might give such a wink to a German.

— And I remember, me, said Gerbier, brutally clenching his jaw, I remember the look of the last German I saw …

— Eh, well? Jardie asked.

— They were eyes like snakeskin, said Gerbier. The eyes of the S.S. man who forced me to run. I swear that if you'd been in my place …

— But for you, my old Gerbier, I wouldn't hesitate a second, cried Jardie. I would've saved myself like a rabbit, like a poor rabbit, and without shame, and I wouldn't have seen my boss, as you did, nor the candles of London. I would've been so afraid …

Jardie laughed with a silent fullness that made him seem like a child again. Then he said seriously:

— You've no idea, Gerbier, how wonderful you are.

Gerbier began to pace the room.

— Here we are far from the solution to our problem, Jardie suddenly said.

— It depends on the mail, said Gerbier.

— The Bison must've arrived, but I needed to talk with you at some length, said Jardie.

Gerbier went toward the vestibule.

— It's useless for the Bison to know that I'm here, said Jardie. He went into the adjoining room and quietly closed the door.

VII

The Bison entered, and, behind him, Jean-François. The Bison gave Gerbier a pack of cigarettes.

— You miss it, I'm sure, he said.

Gerbier didn't answer. His hands trembled a bit when tearing open the bluish paper. He breathed in the first puffs with famished avidity. Then he asked, "Mathilde?"

The Bison, who had watched Gerbier smoking with a sort of friendly & gross complicity spreading over the entirety of his massive face, became inaccessible in one fell stroke.

— Eh, well? Gerbier asked impatiently.

— I know nothing, said the Bison.

— And your surveillance team? Gerbier asked.

The Bison bowed slightly toward the ground & his narrow forehead was riddled with deep wrinkles.

— I know nothing, he said.

Gerbier tried to catch his eyes but couldn't make contact.

The Bison put his fist under his flattened nose and muttered between his teeth & his clenched fingers:

— I don't know anything. Everything's in the mail.

He handed over the sheets of thin paper covered with minuscule text written in code. Gerbier lit a cigarette with the one that was burning in his mouth and he began to work. Jean-François and the Bison were standing silently in the shadow. That lasted a long time. Finally Gerbier raised his head. It was right under the lamp.

The circle of light accentuated his sudden sharp facial features in a strange manner.

— Mathilde was freed the day before yesterday and Gerbonnel, Arnaud, and Roux were arrested, said Gerbier.

Gerbier turned to the Bison and asked him:

— Okay? …

— Well, it's in the mail, said the Bison.

His voice was even rougher than usual.

Gerbier turned toward Jean-François:

— You knew it … he asked.

— I wasn't in charge of the report, said Jean-François.

Gerbier felt that those two men, the most loyal, the most trustworthy, the toughest, were being evasive. And he felt that in their place that he would have had the same attitude. It's precisely why he was suddenly freed from any inner struggle, free of all scruples, and free of any pity. He told the Bison bluntly and in a tone that always commands obedience:

— Mathilde is to be liquidated, with extreme urgency, &
by whatever means ...

— It isn't true, said the Bison. He shook his forehead low
and continued in one breath:

— No, I will not touch Madame Mathilde. I worked with
her. I was saved by her. I saw her polishing off the Gestapo
with a tommy gun. She's a great woman. Men, when necessary ... anything you say ... But Madame Mathilde, as long
as I'm alive ... never.

Gerbier relit his cigarette and said:

— There's nothing to argue over — she must disappear.
She will disappear ...

— You won't do that, said the Bison.

— We have other killers besides you, said Gerbier, shrugging his shoulders. And if necessary, it'll be me ...

— You won't do it, the Bison whispered; you've no right ...
I tell you. On the shooting range, you could've run like a
champion and you'd still be at the mass grave right now without Madame Mathilde, who found the grenades.

Gerbier's face lost all expression. The Bison drew close to
him. His terrible form emerged from the shadows.

— You won't do it, he said. She can sell all of us out, if she
wants. She defended me. She defended you. Now she defends
her daughter. It's not for us to judge.

The Bison was speaking very low. His voice was danger-
ously beseeching.

— Enough ... said Gerbier. The question is settled. Since
you don't want to do it, I'll put a note in the mail.

The Bison spoke in an even lower voice:

— If you're craven enough to do it, you'll go down first, he said.

Gerbier began to write.

Near him, under the lamp, the face of the Bison assumed such an expression that Jean-François grabbed his wrist.

— You won't touch a boss, he whispered.

— Go away, said the Bison, and do it quickly… You've nothing to teach me. You were playing marbles when I was commanding men in the Legion. Get out of my face, I tell you … or you'll both be done for.

Jean-François knew the muscular power of the Bison. He recoiled and pulled out his rubber truncheon. Gerbier's hand was poised on his revolver in the table drawer.

VIII

— I believe that we need a man who knows nothing about weapons in this uninhabited house, said Jardie.

Gerbier didn't turn around. Jean-François reflexively drew up beside his brother. The Bison retreated into the depths of the shadow. He had seen Jardie only once, but he knew that he was the boss.

— My friend, sit down, Jardie said to him. And you too, he said to Jean-François.

Jardie took a chair and added:

— Now light a cigarette. It's very good, they tell me. Is it not, Gerbier? …

He finally turned round.

— You heard everything? he asked.

Jardie didn't answer him and addressed the Bison.

— You're right, he said, Mathilde is a wonderful woman. Even more than you think … But we'll kill her.

The Bison murmured:

— It isn't possible.

— But if, but if … Jardie said. You will see, my friend. We will kill Mathilde because she begs us to.

— Did she tell you that? the Bison quickly asked.

— No, but it's clear all the same, said Jardie. Think about it a little bit. If Mathilde had simply wanted to save her daughter, all she had to do was to hand over a list of names & addresses. You know her memory …

— Astounding, said the Bison.

— All right, Jardie said. Instead of doing that, Mathilde tells them that our people constantly change addresses … That she has to reestablish contacts … anything whatsoever. In brief, she gets herself set free. Isn't it clear enough?

The Bison didn't answer. He swung his head from right to left & left to right.

— Suppose that you were in Mathilde's place, that you were OBLIGED to give up your friends, and you don't have the means to commit suicide …

— I'd want to be put out of the way, it's true, said the Bison slowly.

Jardie himself laughed.

— So, you think that you're braver & better than Mathilde? he asked.

The Bison became very red:

— You must excuse me, boss, he said.

— Well, Jardie said. You will take a German car, little Jean will drive, and I will be with you in the back seat.

Gerbier made such a fast movement that the lamp flickered.

— Boss, what is this madness? he asked dryly.

— I'm sure that Mathilde will be pleased to see me, said Jardie.

Jean-François murmured:

— I beg you — it isn't your place, Saint Luc.

Because his brother had rediscovered his old nickname, Jardie put his hand on his shoulder and he laughed, with more friendliness than usual:

— It's an order.

— There was no need for that, boss, said the Bison.

Gerbier wrote out the message. The Bison took it & left. Jean-François exited on a sign from his brother.

IX

— You're sure about what you've claimed about Mathilde? Gerbier asked.

— How can I tell … said Jardie.

He twirled a white tuft between his fingers.

— It's possible that this hypothesis may be correct, he said. It's also possible that Mathilde had wanted to see her children and that she has become more difficult to kill. This is what I want to find out.

Gerbier shuddered & whispered low:

— You, in that car of killers ... There's nothing sacred left in this world.

He didn't even think to conceal the agitation of his lower jaw.

— I stayed with you for what was most important, said Jardie. London requests a man from among us for some consultations. You'll make the first trip.

Gerbier dog-eared the corner of a card.

— It's a convalescent leave? he asked.

Jardie laughed & said:

— You still don't want to run, Gerbier? ...

— Oh! this time I good and well want to, said Gerbier.

He felt a miserable & all-powerful joy flow through his body.

X

When Mathilde saw the car of killers approach her, Jardie could make out nothing from her face.

The Bison fired as usual, without fault.

And Jean-François managed to elude the pursuers.

Gerbier spent three weeks in London.

He left again for France, healthy and very calm.

He regained the use of his half-smile.

London, September 1943

COLOPHON

ARMY OF SHADOWS

was handset in InDesign CC.

The text & page numbers are set in *Adobe Jenson Pro*.
The titles are set in *Berliner Grotesk*.

Book design & typesetting: Alessandro Segalini
Cover design: Rainer J. Hanshe & Alessandro Segalini

ARMY OF SHADOWS

is published by Contra Mundum Press.
Its printer has received Chain of Custody certification from:
The Forest Stewardship Council,
The Programme for the Endorsement of Forest Certification,
& The Sustainable Forestry Initiative.

Contra Mundum Press   New York · London · Melbourne

CONTRA MUNDUM PRESS

Dedicated to the value & the indispensable importance of the individual voice, to works that test the boundaries of thought & experience.

The primary aim of Contra Mundum is to publish translations of writers who in their use of form and style are *à rebours*, or who deviate significantly from more programmatic & spurious forms of experimentation. Such writing attests to the volatile nature of modernism. Our preference is for works that have not yet been translated into English, are out of print, or are poorly translated, for writers whose thinking & æsthetics are in opposition to timely or mainstream currents of thought, value systems, or moralities. We also reprint obscure and out-of-print works we consider significant but which have been forgotten, neglected, or overshadowed.

There are many works of fundamental significance to *Weltliteratur* (& *Weltkultur*) that still remain in relative oblivion, works that alter and disrupt standard circuits of thought — these warrant being encountered by the world at large. It is our aim to render them more visible.

For the complete list of forthcoming publications, please visit our website. To be added to our mailing list, send your name and email address to: info@contramundum.net

Contra Mundum Press
P.O. Box 1326
New York, NY 10276
USA

Printed in the USA
CPSIA information can be obtained
at www.ICGtesting.com
CBHW030942061123
1699CB00004B/37